三

What Jesus Said About...

What Jesus Said About...

Morris L. Venden

Pacific Press Publishing Association
Mountain View, California
Oshawa, Ontario

Designed by Ichiro Nakashima

Copyright © 1984 by
Pacific Press Publishing Association
Printed in United States of America

Library of Congress Cataloging in Publication Data

Venden, Morris L.
  What Jesus said about.
  1. Seventh-Day Adventists—Doctrines. 2. Jesus Christ—
Teachings.   I. Title.
BX6154.V44   1984   230'.673   83-26287
ISBN 0-8163-0555-2

Contents

Introduction 9
What Jesus Said About Justification 13
What Jesus Said About the Faith Relationship 23
What Jesus Said About Himself 37
What Jesus Said About Sanctification 49
What Jesus Said About Perfection 65
What Jesus Said About the Investigative Judgment 75
What Jesus Said About Prophets 91
What Jesus Said About Devil Possession 101
What Jesus Said About the Mismanagement of Church Funds 115
What Jesus Said About the Atonement 123

INTRODUCTION

The Bible was not written simply for the purpose of challenging the scholar or the theologian to greater intellectual achievements. In fact, we are told that "the Bible with its precious gems of truth was not written for the scholar alone. On the contrary, it was *designed* for the common people; and the interpretation given by the common people, *when aided by the Holy Spirit,* accords best with the truth as it is in Jesus. The great truths necessary for salvation are made clear as the noonday, and none will mistake and lose their way except those who follow their own judgment instead of the plainly revealed will of God."—*Testimonies,* vol. 5, p. 331. Emphasis supplied.

So the Bible is designed to be studied and understood by everybody. And within the Bible, there is no clearer portrayal of truth than can be found in the teachings of Jesus. "No other light has ever shone or ever will shine so clearly upon fallen man as that which emanated from the teaching and example of Jesus."—*The Desire of Ages,* p. 220.

So if you are looking for light and truth on any subject, one of the best places to start is to look at the life and teachings of Jesus, who was the Word of God in human form. "In the beginning was the Word, and the Word was with God, and the Word was God. The same was in the beginning with God. All things were made by him; and without him was not any thing made that was made." "And the Word was made flesh, and dwelt among us, (and we beheld his glory, the glory as of the only begotten of the Father), full of grace and truth." John 1:1-3, 14.

Have you ever gone through a book with the specific purpose

of trying to find out everything you can on one particular topic? It is a very effective trick for keeping your attention, and it also can be a helpful tool in gathering together all of the available information on a particular topic from what you are reading. When the discussions and debates were on the rise within the church in recent years, some of us became frustrated with trying to listen and study and decide for ourselves what was truth and what was falsehood with respect to the various subjects that were being bandied about. After a time of frustration, we turned to the life and teachings of Christ, and in following a systematic study of the four Gospels, along with the inspired commentary on the four Gospels, we developed a study guide, *Countdown Desire*. This study guide of the life and teachings of Christ deliberately attempts to allow room for each person's individual interests as he studies.

This book is a sequel to that study, giving a synopsis, which *Countdown Desire* does not, and leading to conclusions on what Jesus had to say on ten of the major topics that have been under discussion within the church in recent times.

We shall notice what Jesus said regarding Himself, sanctification, perfection, the investigative judgment, the prophets, casting out demons, giving in spite of mismanagement of church funds, and the atonement.

May you be drawn closer to Him and come to know Him better, as you examine what He had to say about the issues that face us today.

Satan's original charge was that the law of God could not be obeyed. When man broke the law of God, Satan exulted and added another charge–that man could not be forgiven. He had no idea that God Himself would pay the penalty. But Jesus' life and death proved that sinners could be forgiven and that the law of God can be obeyed, not only by Jesus, but by those who live the life of faith as He did. This twofold message of forgiveness and obedience is the heart of the remnant's mission during the time of the three angels and the final work of Christ in heaven. Jesus as our High Priest provides forgiveness for sinners and power to obey. These two truths are equally necessary. It is extremely important that the remnant people understand this twofold work of Christ in heaven; otherwise, it will be impossible for them to fulfill their mission. Justification by faith (God's work for us) and the righteousness of Christ (which includes God's work in us) are the themes to be presented to a perishing world.

What Jesus Said About Justification

Justification is the foundation truth in the study of salvation by faith alone. Jesus came to offer us pardon, forgiveness, and acceptance with the Father because of His merits. Matthew 1:21 introduces Jesus as the One who "shall save his people from their sins." Jesus is uplifted as "the Lamb of God, which taketh away the sin of the world." John 1:29. The Pharisees and scribes spoke the truth when they said, "This man receiveth sinners." Luke 15:2.

Jesus came not to call the righteous, but sinners to repentance. See Matthew 9:13. He came to seek and save that which was lost. See Luke 19:10. Repeatedly in His contact with the people of His day, He assured them that He forgave them, that He accepted them, and that He did not condemn them. See John 3:17; Luke 5:20-24; John 8:11; Luke 7:48.

Let's look in a little more detail at the story Jesus told of one sinner who was justified, found in Luke 18:9-14. "And he spake this parable unto certain which *trusted in themselves* that they were righteous, and despised others. Two men went up into the temple to pray, the one a Pharisee, and the other a publican. The Pharisee stood and prayed thus *with himself,* God, I thank thee, that I am not as other men are, extortioners, unjust, adulterers, or even as this publican. I fast twice in the week"—the Pharisee was probably slim and trim. "I give tithes of all that I possess"—the church that he attended was probably financially secure. But "the publican, standing afar off, would not lift up so much as his eyes unto heaven, but smote upon his breast, saying, God be merciful to me a sinner." (Some other versions say, "God be merciful to me *the* sinner.") "I tell you, this man went down to his house *justified* rather than the other: for every one that exalteth himself shall be abased; and he that humbleth himself shall be exalted." Emphasis supplied.

We notice first of all that this parable was spoken for certain which trusted in themselves. The primary group to which this parable was intended was the Pharisees—the tithepayers, people who practiced fasting at regular intervals. Notice that both the Pharisee and the publican went to the temple to worship, but only one really worshiped, because you can't worship God and yourself at the same time. Only one worshiped God. They both went there to pray. Only one really prayed. It says the Pharisee prayed with himself. He wasn't praying to God.

And the Pharisee reminds us of what Jesus said in Matthew 9:13, "I am not come to call the righteous, but sinners to repentance." And He said in Matthew 5:20, "Unless your righteousness shall exceed the righteousness of the . . . Pharisees," there's no hope that you will enter heaven. The problem of the Pharisee was that he had the idea he could save himself. And there is a warning against this. Anyone who thinks that he can save himself is becoming his own god. And for someone to become his own god, or his own saviour, is the same thing as trying to take the place of God. The hardest-hitting warnings in all of Scripture, particularly in Revelation, are against doing this. Someone who tries to take the place of God is called a blasphemer. See John 10:33. Blasphemers do not get very good marks in Scripture, in fact, it borders on the unpardonable sin.

We also notice, when we study incidents in Jesus' life, that the next step for the person who is trying to save himself is to forsake Jesus. We read, for instance, in Matthew 26:51-56 that Peter drew his sword to try to save himself. And the very next thing that happened was that "they all [including Peter] forsook him, and fled." They ran from Jesus. This is inevitably what happens to anyone who tries to save himself. In the end, he will leave Jesus.

The story of the Pharisee and the publican reminds us that salvation is a gift. It isn't something we can secure by our fasting or by our tithing or by anything else that we consider makes us righteous. Salvation is a gift. Jesus said, concerning the temple where these two came to worship, that everything should be taken out that would make His house a house of merchandise. There's something deeper here than just talking about doves and pigeons and lambs. God's house is not a marketplace; it is a true *gift* shop. Salvation cannot be bought or sold. And Jesus said in Luke 14:14 that those who cannot pay are the ones who are recompensed at the resurrection. In other words, they are the ones who are invited to the gospel feast. In fact, Matthew 22:10 says that even bad people are invited—you remember that the king's servants invited both bad and good. And the Bible has something to say about how many good there are. How many? Not one. So the only thing you have left is for bad people to be invited to the gospel feast.

In the story of the Pharisee and the publican we have clear evidence that we need a substitute, someone to take our place. Even Christ's enemies confirmed this fact. Caiaphas said, as recorded in John 11:50, "It is expedient for us, that one man should die for the people, and that the whole nation perish not." And the apostle John comments, in verses 51 and 52, "And this spake he not of himself: but being high priest that year, he prophesied that Jesus should die for that nation; and not for that nation only, but that also he should gather together in one the children of God that were scattered abroad." Jesus said it of Himself, in 1 Corinthians 11:24, "This is my body, which is broken *for you.*" Emphasis supplied. John 10:9-11 says that the Good Shepherd gives His life *for* the sheep.

If it had been possible for the Pharisee, in any way, to bring something in his hand, to earn or merit God's grace or favor, this would have immediately diminished the sacrifice, wouldn't it? The death of Jesus as our Substitute will be discussed in greater detail in chapter 10, "What Jesus Said About the Atonement." But salvation is totally a gift of Jesus Christ; it is not based in any way on our own merits.

Now let us consider the publican. The publican realized that there was nothing he could do. There was no way he could add anything to the salvation provided. One of the reasons he recognized this was that he recognized himself as a terrible sinner. We could title his story, "Salvation for the Worst Man on Earth."

And if salvation doesn't include the worst man on earth, it's no good, is it?

Notice the publican. He stands afar off, an indication that he feels under conviction. He doesn't even dare to lift his eyes unto heaven. Evidently he was feeling condemned. But it wasn't overwhelming condemnation, because if it were, he wouldn't even have shown up at the temple, would he? He is a man who is convicted, who feels under condemnation, because he can't hold his head up. And so he stands there, feeling a sense of sinfulness, but with some hope—that's why he came.

And then he says, God, be merciful to me, *the* sinner. Not merely *a* sinner, as the KJV translates it. It would be one thing to say, I am *a* sinner. But to say I am *the* sinner, the number one sinner, the worst man in the world, that's something else. Do you have to be that bad in order to make this kind of confession? Do you have to have a terrible track record? Do you have to be scooped out of the gutter? Paul wasn't. He was a Pharisee of the Pharisees. He had a blameless life, but one day he was willing to say, I am the chief of sinners. See 1 Timothy 1:15. Isn't that the position God invites all of us to come to—I am the sinner?

But words come cheap, you know. Words really come cheap. There is a syndrome in Christian circles where people don't feel good unless they feel sinful. There is a very subtle system of penance and works, where legalism crops out and we mouth the words that we think are supposed to be mouthed. But there's a lot of difference between taking security in your penitence, and in *being* penitent, because the Holy Spirit has brought you there. Notice that the publican does not say, "God be merciful to me because of my penitence." It's "God be merciful to me the sinner." He was penitent, no question about that. But he didn't make his salvation dependent upon his penitence.

People sometimes like to discuss which comes first, repentance or forgiveness. There is a sense in which forgiveness must be preceded by repentance. There is another sense in which it is God's forgiveness that brings us to repentance. When Peter denied his Lord, we are told that Jesus turned and looked at him, there in the courtyard, and that look of Christ assured him of pardon. See *Christ's Object Lessons,* p. 154. It was

JUSTIFICATION

that look of compassion and forgiveness that pierced Peter's heart like an arrow, aroused conscience, and caused him to rush heartbroken from the hall. It was that look of forgiveness that broke his heart and led him to repentance. The same thing will happen to us as we behold the Lamb of God, and the cross of Calvary, and as the mystery of redemption begins to unfold in our minds. God's goodness will lead us to repentence. See *Steps to Christ,* p. 26.

So which comes first? Well, it depends on your point of view. Forgiveness is a gift. But it is more than a gift; it is an experience. The experience of forgiveness is impossible without repentance. Perhaps we could say that the possibility of forgiveness, the assurance of forgiveness, is what leads to repentance. But it is the Holy Spirit that brings both. Neither one is something we can do for ourselves. Both are gifts from Jesus, and neither of them can be experienced apart from Jesus.

So, if I want to stand in the shoes of the publican and not just mouth the words of repentance, what should I do? Must I wait until the right preacher comes along, with the right kind of powerful appeal? There's something far bigger than that! We can deliberately choose to study everything available about what Jesus has already done for us, and it will break our hearts.

The next thing we notice in this story is that the publican who came in this fashion was accepted. And here is a key word in the entire beautiful theme of justification. *Acceptance* is the word. As you study what Jesus had to say and how He treated people, you can't miss the conclusion that we are always accepted just as we are. That's the only way we can come to Jesus. We cannot change ourselves in order to come to Him.

This is true not only at the beginning of the Christian life, but it is true every day of the Christian life as well. Jesus loves to accept us just as we are. Jesus said in John 6:37, "Him that cometh to me I will in no wise cast out." Jesus said in John 7:37, "If any man thirst, let him come unto me, and drink." And this loving acceptance carries with it no condemnation. Jesus said it in John 3:17, "God sent not his Son into the world to condemn the world; but that the world through him might be saved." Jesus said it in John 8:11 to the woman the scribes and Pharisees dragged to Him, "I don't condemn you." Jesus said it in John 5:24, "I came not to judge the world but to save the world." And Jesus said it in John 5:24, "Verily, verily, I say unto you, He that heareth my word, and believeth on him that sent me, *hath* everlasting life, and shall not come into condemnation." Emphasis supplied. It says that those who hear His word will not even come into judgment, but are passed from death unto life.

Isn't it good news to know that we don't have to fear the judgment? This acceptance is full and free; it is based upon what Jesus has done. It's good for every day, and it causes a poor publican, who can't even get into the back row, or even lift his eyes up to heaven, to be able to go home to his house on the other side of town, holding his head high, because he realizes he is worth everything in the eyes of the universe. Not only is he accepted, but he is also forgiven as well. That's good news.

Jesus said of the publican in this story, "This man went down to his house *justified*." Well, what kind of forgiveness is this and how long does it last and how long do we need it? Let's read three texts in a row that are very pertinent to this whole question of forgiveness. The first is found in Matthew 18:21. "Then Peter came to him, and said, Lord, how often shall my brother sin against me, and I forgive him? till seven times? Jesus saith unto him, I say not unto thee, Until seven times: but, Until seventy times seven." What does this mean? Jesus isn't saying to forgive 490 times and then forget it—but rather to forgive your brother so long as he keeps asking. Isn't that right?

Now let's go to the second text, Luke 17:3-5, and find how much deeper this goes. "Take heed to yourselves: If thy brother trespass against thee, rebuke him; and if he repent forgive him. And if he trespass against thee seven times in a day—" Wait a minute! Do you mean that if I offend you, and I ask you to forgive me, and you forgive me, and it happens seven times in the same day, you are still supposed to forgive me? Will you go for that? Or will you have me in court by the end of the day?

"And if he trespass against thee seven times in a day, and seven times in a day turn again to thee, saying, I repent; thou shalt forgive him. And the apostles said unto the Lord, Increase our faith." I think that every one of us would express the same need, wouldn't we?

JUSTIFICATION 19

But these texts remind us of what kind of forgiveness God has for us, because God would not ask us to be more forgiving among ourselves than He is of us. Please—this *is* God's forgiveness. This is the way God forgives.

Of course, right here some people get nervous, afraid that this is going to lead to license. That's why some people are nervous about the theme of justification. But we have to add our third text—the proof against license—Luke 7:40-43.

It happened at the feast in Simon's house. Simon had been inwardly condemning Mary and wondering why Jesus did not condemn her. "And Jesus answering said unto him, Simon, I have somewhat to say unto thee. And he saith, Master, say on. There was a certain creditor which had two debtors: the one owed him five hundred pence, and the other fifty. And when they had nothing to pay, he frankly forgave them both. Tell me therefore, which of them will love him most? Simon answered and said, I suppose he, to whom he forgave the most. And he said unto him, Thou hast rightly judged."

All right, so Jesus said to forgive unendingly. He's saying that for anyone who comes, and keeps coming, His Father's forgiveness is unending. Will this lead to license? No, because the more you are forgiven, the more you love. And John 14:15, RSV, says: "If you love me, you will keep my commandments." So if we really understand God's forgiveness, it does not lead us to play loose with God's grace, but leads to love, and love leads to obedience. It's just that simple.

What does the forgiveness of God include? Let's read it from *Steps to Christ,* page 62. "He died for us, and now He offers to take our sins and give us His righteousness. If you give yourself to Him, and accept Him as your Saviour, then, sinful as your life may have been, for His sake you are accounted righteous. Christ's character stands in place of your character, and you are accepted before God just as though you had not sinned." God's brand of forgiveness is far more than forgiveness! When you forgive me, you can still remember the words I used to offend you. But when God forgives me, I stand before Him as though I had never even sinned.

How long will I need this forgiveness? Listen, friend, don't fall into the trap of thinking that justification is only for the beginning of our Christian lives. We need God's justifying grace every day. That's part of the reason we need a day-by-day relationship with Jesus. We need to come to Him each day through Bible study and prayer and accept His justifying grace. We need His justification because of our past track record, whether we ever sin again or not. We need His justifying grace because we have sinful natures, and will continue to have sinful natures until Jesus comes again.

So the publican went down to his house justified. And that's good news for us today, because Jesus said, "Blessed are they which do hunger and thirst after righteousness: for they shall be filled." Matthew 5:6. He said to His disciples in the upper room, before Peter denied Him, "Now are ye clean." John 15:3. Did that mean the disciples would never fall or fail again? No, but they were clean, through what Jesus had done and was doing for them.

Does this bring peace? Yes, it brings peace. Jesus said, "These things I have spoken unto you, that in me ye might have peace." John 16:33. "Take my yoke upon you, and learn of me . . . ; and ye shall find rest unto your souls." Matthew 11:29. "If the Son shall make you free, ye shall be free indeed." John 8:36. Peace with God? No question about it. Jesus still offers His peace to us today.

And the result of accepting His peace is that we have certainty and assurance concerning our eternal destiny. The purpose of understanding what He has done for us is to give us this kind of certainty. Go through your Bible one of these days, particularly the book of John, and underline all of the verses that tell you that you *have* eternal life. We already have it! It's not something we are going to get later on—we have it already. John 6:47 and John 6:54 are a couple of examples of this promise. Jesus said to His disciples, "Rejoice, because your names *are* written in heaven." Luke 10:20, RSV. Emphasis supplied. Not, they "will be" written, but, they "are already" written there. He said to Zacchaeus, *"This day* salvation has come to this house." Luke 19:9. Emphasis supplied. And John 20:31 says, "These are written, that ye might believe that Jesus is the Christ, the Son of God; and that believing ye might *have* life through his name." Emphasis supplied.

To many of us, this seems like truth almost too good to be ac-

JUSTIFICATION 21

cepted. But it is still the truth. In 1 John 5:11, 12 we read, "God hath given to us eternal life, and this life is in his Son. He that hath the Son hath life; and he that hath not the Son of God hath not life." This is still true, whether we believe it or not. Is there anyone who is too sinful, who cannot qualify? Is there someone today who says, That may have been good for the publican back there, and it may be good for others, but not for me? Then please read these encouraging words from *Steps to Christ,* pages 52, 53:

"Put away the suspicion that God's promises are not meant for you. They are for every repentant transgressor. Strength and grace have been provided through Christ to be brought by ministering angels to every believing soul. None are so sinful that they cannot find strength, purity, and righteousness in Jesus, who died for them. He is waiting to strip them of their garments stained and polluted with sin, and to put upon them the white robe of His righteousness. He bids them live and not die."

Do you believe that? Do you accept that? It is for you today. You can, today, go to your home, just as did the publican, justified.

(For additional references pertaining to this subject see *Countdown Desire* [Mountain View, Calif.: Pacific Press Publishing Association, 1982], pp. 191-195.)

Satan's original charge was that the law of God could not be obeyed. When man broke the law of God, Satan exulted and added another charge–that man could not be forgiven. He had no idea that God Himself would pay the penalty. But Jesus' life and death proved that sinners could be forgiven and that the law of God can be obeyed, not only by Jesus, but by those who live the life of faith as He did. This twofold message of forgiveness and obedience is the heart of the remnant's mission during the time of the three angels and the final work of Christ in heaven. Jesus as our High Priest provides forgiveness for sinners and power to obey. These two truths are equally necessary. It is extremely important that the remnant people understand this twofold work of Christ in heaven; otherwise, it will be impossible for them to fulfill their mission. Justification by faith (God's work for us) and the righteousness of Christ (which includes God's work in us) are the themes to be presented to a perishing world.

What Jesus Said About the Faith Relationship

When my son was a boy I made him a custom-made bicycle. I worked for hours on it out in the garage in secret, before Christmas Day. It was a gift. It was the best I could do. It was a gift for him, yet it would have been no good for him if he had not accepted it the day I gave it to him. In fact, if he had not accepted it, not only would the gift have done him no good, but it would also have been a slap in my face if he had refused it after my having made it for him.

Regardless of how good or how inferior a gift is, a gift does no good unless it is accepted. If the gift is perfect, rejecting it not only does no good, but it is also a slap in the face of the giver.

As beautiful as the doctrine and the truth of justification is, as beautiful as what God has done for us is, as beautiful as the sacrifice on the cross stands in all of history, it does no good for anybody until it is accepted.

Justification is mankind being put right with God through what Jesus has done. It is a provision in heaven for the redemption of the whole human race. And it has as its foundation the spotless righteousness of Jesus. Justification, however, does no good for any sinner until it is accepted by that sinner. The Bible does not teach that justification is by grace alone; it is always by grace through faith. Faith is essential on the part of the sinner. The greatest single definition of faith is trust. Trust usually involves two parties, one trusting the other. When the sinner trusts Jesus for salvation, there comes into existence a saving relationship. When the sinner accepts salvation by faith, there is more than a legal declaration in heaven; there is the beginning of a relationship with God, followed by ethical results and expectations.

As we pursue what Jesus had to say about this faith relationship, I'd like to suggest that we try to understand clearly the difference between "only believe" and a living, vital relationship. Perhaps you are aware that the nominal Christian world has for years held on to "only believe" as their brand of faith. We have some very specific counsels against this teaching written to our church, and these counsels are based on the premise that "only believe" too often includes merely an intellectual assent to truth, rather than a personal, vital relationship with God. The person who believes that "only believe" is faith, is also the person who does not believe that we can obey God's commandments. The person who believes in a vital relationship with Christ as necessary to produce genuine faith believes that we can obey God's commandments, that there is power available to make us overcomers.

Let's begin with John 17:3, where Jesus goes immediately to the point of what eternal life is all about, what eternal life is based on so far as our reception of it is concerned. John 17:3 says, "This is life eternal, that they might know thee the only true God, and Jesus Christ, whom thou hast sent." Eternal life, obviously, is based upon Jesus and what He has done, but here the emphasis is upon our receiving of it, our acceptance of the gift, the part we have to play in it. We come into this relationship of knowing Him. When we first accept of His mighty grace, at justification, the relationship begins. As we continue to accept of His grace on a daily basis, the relationship continues. And that is just as important as the beginning of a marriage and the continuation of a marriage. It is ridiculous to try to decide which is more important, getting married or staying married. Both are important; both are necessary.

Coming to Jesus is important. Staying with Jesus is important. They are both important. One is an illustration of justification; the other is an illustration of continuing justification and sanctification, accepting His grace on a daily basis. It's one thing for my boy to ride his bike Christmas Day and never touch it again. It's another thing for me to realize that he likes the bike as he rides it every day. And so, Jesus said, eternal life, so far as we are concerned, is to come into that saving relationship with Him.

He contrasts this very clearly in two other texts, showing why some people will be lost. Matthew 25:1-13, the story of the ten young women in the wedding party, leads to this conclusion. Five had asked to be admitted to the banquet, and the answer was given, I know you not. Their problem was that they did not have a personal relationship with God. The other text is in the same book, Matthew 7:23, where once again it is stated clearly, "Then will I profess unto them, I never knew you: depart from me, ye that work iniquity." Had they been working iniquity? Notice what they had done. They had said, "Lord, Lord." Verse 22. They knew how to mouth the name of Jesus. They had been involved in prophesying, they had cast out devils, and they had done many wonderful works. Yet Jesus said, It is all iniquity. Why? Because they didn't know Him. So evidently it is possible through some other power to do all of these things and still not know God, not know Jesus Christ.

There it is in a nutshell, and I suppose we could close the chapter right here. Jesus made it clear that your eternal life and mine is based upon knowing Him and what He has done for us. And those who are lost will be those who don't know Him. That means there are only two kinds of people in the world—those who know God and those who don't know God. Those who know God have accepted His justifying grace and continue to accept it day by day. And those who don't know God either have not accepted of His grace, or have once accepted, but have done nothing about it ever since. It's true that some people became Christians twenty years ago and have done nothing about it since, just like some people were married twenty years ago and have done nothing about that since.

Now let us consider the question of faith, because we are looking at these two topics together—faith and relationship—as being one and the same thing, in a sense. There is no faith, no saving faith, without this relationship. And there is no relationship without faith. What is faith? The next time you go through the four Gospels—Matthew, Mark, Luke, and John—susbstitute the word *trust* every time you come to the word *belief* or *faith*. You will find that the clearest definition of faith is trust. The reason it helps us to look at faith as trust is because a relationship is required in order for someone to trust another.

If I want to develop genuine faith or trust, then the way to go about learning to trust someone is to get to know them. If we get acquainted with one who is truthworthy, we will trust him spontaneously. And the way we get acquainted is to communicate, which is where life eternal, as far as our acceptance of it is concerned, comes in. How can we know God? In the same way by which we can know anyone. We get acquainted with someone by talking to them, by listening to them, and by going places and doing things with them. So if we are going to put faith and relationship together and look at the common denominator of both, we discover that trust, developed through fellowship and communion, is the essence of the whole matter.

If you are going to look in the Bible for the basis of the ongoing relationship with God, you will find it in John 17:3—"that they might know thee the only true God." The great Bible truth is that faith is never something we work on. It isn't something we conjure up in our minds through some sort of mental gymnastics. Faith is always spontaneous and comes as a result of knowing God. The person who does not know God does not have faith. And we have this saving faith only so long as we know God as our personal Friend in a one-to-one relationship.

That brings us to the question of sin. What is the problem in sin, anyway? How did it all begin? It originated from a lack of trust. The essence of sin was a broken relationship. The originator of sin decided that he did not need to trust God, his Creator, anymore. And when he introduced sin into this world, that was still the issue. It wasn't merely a matter of doing bad things, it wasn't merely bad behavior or performance, it was basically a broken relationship.

When a person has lost his relationship with Christ, he also, as far as God is concerned, has lost righteousness. The Bible truth is that there is no such thing as righteousness apart from Jesus. It comes with Him. When I do not have Him, I have no righteousness. When I enter again into a relationship with Him, then righteousness comes through that relationship with Him. Jesus said this in John 16:8, 9, when He declared that when the Holy Spirit came, He would reprove the world of sin, of righteousness, and of judgment. And then He added, "Of sin, because they believe not on me." Substitute *trust* for *believe*—"Of sin, because they trust not in me."

Many theological disputes revolve around the question of whether we sin because we are sinners or whether we are sinners because we sin. But one thing is certain: no one can see the kingdom of God unless he is born again. See John 3:3. But, if this is true, then there must be something wrong with our first birth. The problem with our first birth is that "our hearts are evil, and we cannot change them."—*Steps to Christ,* p. 18. Thus we are faced with the reality of original sin. (I'd like to define original sin here. I'm not talking about the Augustinian brand of original sin, which carries with it original guilt. I'm talking about the Augsburg Confession brand of original sin, which says basically that mankind is born separated from God.) Because of Adam's sin, all of us since that time are born separated from God, as far as any spiritual relationship goes. We are all born separated from God and would have remained so forever, if it had not been for the cross, which gave us another chance. But that option still has to be accepted by us. The practical result of our being born separated from God is that we are born hopelessly self-centered. And this self-centeredness causes all the sins or transgressions that follow.

The problem of sin has even infiltrated the animal kingdom. This fact was brought home to me one night when I heard a couple of "sinners" caterwauling in the woods behind my house. They had four legs and fur. They made quite a preparation as they worked themselves up for their fight, tails flailing the air. You could hear them all over the neighborhood. As I lay awake listening, I winced as I heard them clinch for the "kill." And why were they fighting? Because they were self-centered. You get the point.

The logical conclusion to the idea that we are born self-centered is that a person sins because he is sinful. He is not sinful because he sins. What did Jesus have to say about that? He said very simply in John 3, that we cannot see the kingdom of heaven unless we are born again. Those words, simple as they are, lead us to the conclusion that there is something wrong with every one of us born into this world. If I define sin only in the legalistic understanding, that no one is sinful until he sins, then this will lead me into all kinds of misconceptions concerning the great theme of salvation.

We are all sinners because we were all born sinful. Then what happens at the new birth? What happens when a person realizes his great need and comes to Jesus, acknowledging the fact that in Jesus is his only hope for this world or the next? What is the new birth?

There was a week of prayer several years ago, held by a medical doctor from Loma Linda. I still remember his topic: "What's New About the New Birth?" I like the amplification on the point found in *The Desire of Ages,* from the chapters on Nicodemus and the woman at the well. The new birth is a supernatural work of the Holy Spirit, which produces a change of attitude toward God and creates a new capacity for knowing God that we didn't even have before. At the new birth we are given a capacity for relationship, and if it wasn't for this supernatural work, we wouldn't even have the equipment needed to enter into the relationship with Jesus. This capacity is increased as we continue in our fellowship and communion with God. So the new birth is absolutely essential. The new birth takes place simultaneously with the acceptance of justification, and it gives us the capacity for a vital relationship with God, from which genuine faith springs.

I'll never forget trying to convert my son. He was in the academy, and I was worried about him. At the school where he was going at that time, there were kids who were into drugs, and were supplying drugs to others on campus. When such things are going on, you worry about your son or daughter. And you do everything you can to try to convert them, until you realize that you can't do it. No one can convert someone else. Only the Holy Spirit can do that. I believe that if we'd do less talking and more praying, we'd get further. I have to confess that I talked too much, and when my son didn't even look at me at the breakfast table the next day, I decided I'd better stop talking and do more praying.

Then the kids from the academy (some of those who were not "squares") invited my son to a discussion at the Bible teacher's house. He went with the idea of asking some hard questions. He liked to ask these kinds of questions. Halfway through the evening, something said to him, "Venden, why don't you shut up? Maybe you'll learn something." At that time he didn't know that some of those academy kids were praying for him. I'm thankful for those academy kids! Before the rest of the evening was over, my son listened to something that he'd never paid much attention to before. But he sure *had* heard it before! Would you like to know what he listened to? That we never change our lives in order to come to Jesus. We always come to Jesus just as we are, and He's the one who changes our lives. I can't tell you how often he had heard that before, but somehow had never gotten through to him.

He came home, about ready to speak in tongues, he was so excited. He said, "Look, Dad! Listen to this! We never change our lives in order to come to Christ. We come just as we are, and He loves to have us come just as we are. And He's the one who changes our lives."

I didn't want to spoil his enthusiasm so I said, "Really? Tell me more!" And the blood was singing in my veins.

He told me more, and before the week was out, he had an evangelistic meeting in the living room, with as many kids from the academy as he could get to come, trying to convince his friends of the truth that you never change your life in order to come to Christ. You come just as you are, and He's the one who changes your life. His mother and I were in the back room, lying on the floor, listening through the crack under the door!

Listen, friend, if we ever come to Jesus, we're going to have to come just as we are. Whatever else you hear in the present dialogue on salvation by faith, that is one point you can nail down with a sledge hammer. Jesus loves to have us come to Him just as we are. I'm thankful for that kind of Saviour, aren't you?

The morning before my son was converted, he couldn't have cared less about the Bible. The morning after, he couldn't put it down. As I went past his room and looked in, I said to myself, "It's happened." I wanted to sing the doxology—"Praise God, from whom all blessings flow." There is a difference, isn't there? When you come to Christ, you are given a new capacity, and you can tell the difference. It's real.

But it doesn't end there. Spiritual life must go on. It won't do to make a start and let it end right there. Conversion is only the beginning. If only we could get our young people to remember that. Jesus said it again and again—"Abide in me." It seemed to be a favorite phrase of His. What does it mean to abide? It means to stay. It isn't just coming to Him; it's staying with Him. That's what this relationship of faith is all about.

In John 6:53-56 we find some difficult words. "Jesus said unto them, . . . Except ye eat the flesh of the Son of man, and drink his blood, ye have no life in you. Whoso eateth my flesh, and drinketh my blood, hath eternal life; and I will raise him up at the last day." Don't miss that! If we eat His flesh and drink His blood we have eternal life now. "For my flesh is meat indeed, and my blood is drink indeed. He that eateth my flesh, and drinketh my blood, dwelleth in me, and I in him."

I think you'll agree that you can't preach that to cannibals and not be in danger! The people who heard these words of Jesus knew what He was talking about. They knew more than they let on.

Notice the amplification found in *The Desire of Ages,* page 389. "To eat the flesh and drink the blood of Christ is to receive Him as a personal Saviour, believing that He forgives our sins, and that we are complete in Him." That's good news. That's the first part, but notice that it continues. "It is by beholding His love, by dwelling upon it, by drinking it in, that we become partakers of His nature. What food is to the body, Christ must be to the soul. Food cannot benefit us unless we eat it, unless it becomes part of our being. So Christ is of no value to us if we do not know Him as a personal Saviour. A theoretical knowledge will do us no good. We must feed upon Him, receive Him into the heart, so that His life becomes our life."

It was Jesus who is quoted as saying this, and because He said it, we know what it means for us to dwell in Him and He in us. We all know, even without a lot of formal education, that no one can eat for someone else. It would be stupid to try! And yet how often we depend upon someone else for our spiritual food.

So the first part is to receive Jesus, and the second part is to stay with Him and fellowship with Him continually. The relationship that is begun must continue, or His justifying grace will not benefit us.

On one occasion Jesus went to a village in Samaria. He met a woman at the well. After she was convinced that Jesus was the

THE FAITH RELATIONSHIP   31

Messiah, she said to the people of the village, "Come and see." The inspired record says that the whole city came out. Some of them believed the woman, but others who came said, "Now we believe because we have come and seen it for ourselves."

It is never safe to depend upon others for spiritual truth. If you do, sooner or later you are going to go astray. The only safety lies in knowing what it means to study for yourself, to know Christ for yourself, and to determine for yourself what is truth. Except for the Lord Jesus Himself, no one is completely free from error. Let's stop casting about to find someone who has all the truth. We're not going to find such a person. And if you depend upon others, you will go into error as surely as you will die if you depend on someone else to do your eating for you. No one can study and pray and search for someone else.

How do we eat the flesh and drink the blood of the Son of God? It is through the avenues of communication that it happens. Jesus explained the meaning of these words: "The words I speak unto you, they are spirit and they are life." John 6:63. Matthew 4:4 says, "Man shall not live by bread alone, but by every word that proceedeth out of the mouth of God." But there's something deeper than just the words. In the night interview with Nicodemus, Jesus brought him to the realization that he had been studying God's Word for the discussion of a theory. But it is not through controversy and discussion that the soul is enlightened. We must look to Jesus and live. Wouldn't it be tragic if the whole church went down the tubes over discussion and controversy? After his interview with Christ, Nicodemus searched the Scriptures in a new way. He searched not for the discussion of a theory, but for life for his own soul. In order to eat the flesh and drink the blood of Christ, we must study the Bible for the purpose of having a relationship with Christ and deriving spiritual life from Him.

Jesus said in Matthew 26:41, "Watch and pray." He said that whoever loses his life for His sake and the gospel's, will save it. See Mark 8:35. So it is through the channels of communication—His Word, prayer, service for others—that this fellowship continues and we partake of His flesh and blood.

What is the result? According to John 17:20-23, we enter into so close a relationship with Jesus that the Bible describes it as dwelling in Him and He in us. And the result of that is well stated on page 668 of *The Desire of Ages:* "When we know God as it is our privilege to know Him, our life will be a life of continual obedience."

Now I'd like to conclude with this most encouraging truth: although it results in behavior, your relationship with Christ is not based on your behavior. It is based on your response to God's appeal. Anyone who thinks that his relationship with Christ is based upon his behavior will give up that relationship sooner or later. Anyone who becomes discouraged with his relationship with Christ becomes discouraged because he is trying to base his relationship on his behavior. This is nothing more or less than a legalism.

Now there's a difference between getting discouraged over your relationship and in being disappointed in your behavior. I am sometimes disappointed in my behavior, but I am never discouraged with my relationship with Christ! Why? Because Jesus had a way of helping His disciples who fell and sinned again and again. Read about it in Luke 9:55, 56. "He turned, and rebuked them, and said, Ye know not what manner or spirit ye are of. For the Son of man is not come to destroy men's lives, but to save them. And they went to another village." He didn't give them up; He kept on walking with them.

We see this truth in John 3:20, 21. "Every one that doeth evil hateth the light, neither cometh to the light, lest his deeds should be reproved. But he that doeth truth cometh to the light, that his deeds may be manifest, that they are wrought in God." I confess that I didn't see the meaning of that scripture for a long time, until one day it just seemed to jump out at me. I'd like to share it with you. Everyone that does evil hates the light, neither comes to the light. Do any of you feel as if you are doing evil? Maybe that's why you're reading this book—you're looking for help. Do any of you feel that there's not much chance for you to be saved, because of your life, and you don't feel you've been transformed enough, your behavior is not what you know it should be? There's a message here for you.

If a person is really doing evil, in a relationship setting, he won't desire to come to the light. He won't be interested in reading about Jesus. He won't be concerned about going to church or attending other gatherings where Jesus is uplifted. He will have no desire to pray or to search to know God.

But the person who looks forward to attend gatherings where the Bible is studied will find hope in this text. He may still be struggling and making mistakes. But there is provision for the struggling, growing Christian. And there is a sense in which he is not really doing evil, because he is still coming to the light.

Furthermore, for the one who wants supremely to be totally and absolutely surrendered to Christ and who comes to the light at every opportunity, there is a God in heaven who takes notice. And it is He who has put that kind of motivation in your heart in the first place. And, so long as you continue to come to the light, He is able to work in you to accomplish all that He has in mind for your life.

Are you coming to the light today? That is the vital question. And if it wasn't for this realization, many of us would have given up a long time ago.

"The one thing essential for us in order that we may receive and impart the forgiving love of God is to know and believe the love that He has to us. 1 John 4:16. Satan is working by every deception he can command, in order that we may not discern that love. He will lead us to think that our mistakes and transgressions have been so grievous that the Lord will not have respect unto our prayers and will not bless and save us. In ourselves we can see nothing but weakness, nothing to recommend us to God, and Satan tells us that it is of no use; we cannot remedy our defects of character. When we try to come to God, the enemy will whisper, It is of no use for you to pray; did you not do that evil thing? Have you not sinned against God and violated your own conscience? But we may tell the enemy that 'the blood of Jesus Christ His Son cleanseth us from all sin.' 1 John 1:7. When we feel that we have sinned and cannot pray, it is then the time to pray. Ashamed we may be and deeply humbled, but we must pray and believe. 'This is a faithful saying, and worthy of all acceptation, that Christ Jesus came into the world to save sinners; of whom I am chief.' 1 Timothy 1:15. Forgiveness, reconciliation with God, comes to us, not as a reward for our works, it is not bestowed because of the merit of sinful men, but it is a gift unto us, having the spotless righteousness of Christ its foundation for bestowal."—*Thoughts From the Mount of Blessings,* pp. 115, 116.

Take courage, my friend! Jesus continues to walk with you as you continue to fellowship with Him. And sooner or later, His power, which is greater than your failures, will bring you off more than conqueror because of His great love.

(For additional references pertaining to this subject see *Countdown Desire,* pp. 195-199.)

Satan's original charge was that the law of God could not be obeyed. When man broke the law of God, Satan exulted and added another charge–that man could not be forgiven. He had no idea that God Himself would pay the penalty. But Jesus' life and death proved that sinners could be forgiven and that the law of God can be obeyed, not only by Jesus, but by those who live the life of faith as He did. This twofold message of forgiveness and obedience is the heart of the remnant's mission during the time of the three angels and the final work of Christ in heaven. Jesus as our High Priest provides forgiveness for sinners and power to obey. These two truths are equally necessary. It is extremely important that the remnant people understand this twofold work of Christ in heaven; otherwise, it will be impossible for them to fulfill their mission. Justification by faith (God's work for us) and the righteousness of Christ (which includes God's work in us) are the themes to be presented to a perishing world.

What Jesus Said About Himself

Let's face it. Among those who like to talk theology, the subject of the nature of Christ is one of the most devisive and difficult of all. Sometimes we waste endless hours on it, and whole churches have been split over it. And so, it can be very fascinating to find out what Jesus had to say concerning this subject.

For our first scripture let's look at John 14:6-10. "Jesus saith unto him, I am the way, the truth, and the life: no man cometh unto the Father, but by me. If ye had known me, ye should have known my Father also: and from henceforth ye know him, and have seen him. Philip saith unto him, Lord, shew us the Father, and it sufficeth us. Jesus saith unto him, Have I been so long time with you, and yet hast thou not known me, Philip? he that hath seen me hath seen the Father; and how sayest thou then, Shew us the Father? Believest thou not that I am in the Father, and the Father in me? the words that I speak unto you I speak not of myself: but the Father that dwelleth in me, he doeth the works."

This is a very significant passage. It states simply that Jesus was God, that Jesus was man, that He was one with His Father and controlled by His Father, even in the words that He spoke.

Probably all evangelical, fundamental, Bible-believing Christians believe that Jesus was God and is God. We don't have to try to prove that point. It is biblical. But let's notice a few of the major points about it. John 1:1 says, "The Word was with God, and the Word was God." Matthew 3:17, where God Himself is speaking at the baptism of Jesus, says, "This is my beloved Son, in whom I am well pleased." Even the devil knew it, for, according to Matthew 4:3, he tried to tempt Jesus to turn stones into bread. If he didn't know that Jesus was God by birth, that would have been a ridiculous temptation. And not only did the devil know it, but so did all of his imps, for on more than one occasion they said, "We know who You are, the holy one of God."

In John 10:17, 18 Jesus said, I have power to lay down my life, and I have power to take it up again. There's not one of us who could make such a claim. Jesus was talking as God. In Luke 5:20, 21 He showed that He had power to forgive sins, and the scribes and Pharisees charged Him with blasphemy. Once again, Jesus was speaking as God.

In John 13:3 we are told that Jesus knew that He came from God and that He was God. It's very interesting to read the story in *The Desire of Ages* and notice that at age twelve, while He was in the temple, for the first time Jesus realized that He was the One. What an experience that must have been—to wake up to the realization that the Lamb represented Him!

And finally, in Mark 14:61, 62, when they charged Him to speak the truth, under oath He confessed, I am the Son of God.

So Jesus was God. He continued to be God when He became man. And He continues to be God, at the right hand of the Father today. With that in mind, let's proceed to the second main topic under this theme—Jesus was also man. He was human. According to John 1:14, "The Word"—Jesus—"was made flesh, and dwelt among us."

As a man, as a human being, He exhibited certain traits that we are known for. He got tired. See John 4:6. He went to sleep in the bottom of the boat. See Luke 8:23. He got hungry. See Mark 11:12. He got thirsty, and He asked the woman of Samaria for a drink of water (see John 4:7); and He was thirsty again upon the cross (see John 19:28). He found out, as a man, what it is like to experience the necessities that we experience.

Here is where the dialogue and discussions begin in earnest. How much of a man was He? How human was He? Was He just like we are, or was He not? That's where we can take courage from the help we have in the gift that was given to the church, to give us insights into this problem.

If you study carefully *The Desire of Ages,* page 117, you'll discover that Jesus became a man after the race had been degenerating for 4000 years. The race had diminished in physical strength. Jesus got tired when Adam wouldn't have. Jesus fell asleep in the bottom of the boat when perhaps Adam would not have done so. Adam wouldn't even have been in the boat, because he would have sunk the boat! Adam was more than twice as tall as people living today. So Jesus was shorter than Adam. That's an interesting insight.

The race had been degenerating not only in physical strength, but also in mental power. Jesus was not inherently as intelligent as Adam. Apart from God, Adam would have been smarter than Jesus. It sounds almost sacrilegious to say, but it's the truth. Jesus accepted the weakness of humanity in terms of mental power.

And a third area, in which Jesus was weaker than Adam was in moral strength. He didn't have the willpower and backbone to control His actions, apart from God, that Adam would have had. But it made no difference as far as what we see produced in Jesus' life, because He wasn't depending upon willpower. Instead, He was depending upon His Father's divine power—power from above Him. And that made all the difference.

Like His contemporaries, Jesus accepted all the weaknesses of 4000 years of degradation—weaknesses passed on to them by the great law of heredity. See *The Desire of Ages,* p. 49. There is no evidence that sin is passed on through the genes and chromosomes. In other words, just because a man is a drunkard doesn't mean that his son will inevitably be an alcoholic. But a drunkard tends to pass on to his progeny physical, mental, and moral weakness, and because of that, his son will probably be more susceptible to drink. Do you see the difference? Jesus was weakened, not in terms of sins being woven into His genes and chromosomes, but in terms of the fact that He was physically, mentally, and morally weaker than Adam was before he fell. The same is true of all Adam's descendants.

Everyone will agree, I am sure, that Jesus never sinned. In John 8:29, He said this of Himself, "The Father hath not left me alone; for I do always those things that please him." In John 8:46, "Which of you convinceth me of sin?" And before His birth, the angel had said to Mary, "That holy thing which shall be born of thee shall be called the Son of God." Luke 1:35. Jesus was sinless. He was called "that holy thing," and there is no other person ever born in this world called "that holy thing." So we see here a point in which Jesus was born differently from the way we are. He was never a sinner, He never sinned, He was sinless.

Something else that is often debated concerning the humanity of Jesus is whether He was like Adam before the fall or like Adam after the fall. That could keep you going until midnight. Maybe it already has. When you ask the question Was Jesus like Adam before the fall or like Adam after the fall? the answer is Yes to both questions. In some ways Jesus was like Adam before the fall, and in some ways He was like Adam after the fall. The answer becomes complicated because we ask the question in the wrong way. Jesus was like Adam after the fall, as we have already noticed, in terms of physical strength, mental power, and moral worth. But He was like Adam before the fall in that He was sinless.

Jesus had all the liabilities of Adam. See *The Desire of Ages,* p. 117. He could be tempted. He could have given in to temptation. He had a free will. It was possible for Him to fall, to fail, to sin. And yet there was no sin in Him. "No trace of sin marred the image of God within Him [Jesus]. Yet He was not exempt from temptation."—*The Desire of Ages,* p. 71.

What does that mean? It means that He had a nature that carried with it no propensities to sin. That's a big word. We could lose the boys and girls on that one real quick. Let me explain it and define it. The nature of Jesus could be tempted, but it had no cultivated desire for sin. Can you say that about yourself? Of course not. Could this ever be said about anyone else who was born into this world of sin? No.

This leads us to a very practical question: Did Jesus have an advantage over us? The answer is Yes, He did. In Luke 1:35, He is declared to be "that holy thing." This could never be said about any other human being. Unlike us, Jesus was never tempted to *continue* in sin because He never sinned in the first place. From the very outset Jesus hated sin. No other human being can make that claim. So Jesus did have advantages.

But in a sense Jesus had no advantages over us! *The Desire of*

Ages, page 329 states that He knows our weakness by experience. Page 480 tells us that every burden we bear, He has borne. Page 71 points out that He was subject to all our conflicts.

Now how do you get that together? I'd like to suggest that the solution is found in discovering how Jesus lived His life in this world. Page 24 of *The Desire of Ages,* says, "Satan represents God's law of love as a law of selfishness. He declares that it is impossible for us to obey its precepts." Please remember that whenever you hear someone suggest that we cannot obey God's law. That was Satan's charge. The paragraph continues: "Jesus came to unveil this deception. As one of us He was to give us an example of obedience. For this He took upon Himself our nature, and passed through our experience. . . . He endured every trial to which we are subject. And He exercised in His own behalf no power that is not freely offered to us. As man, He met temptation, and overcame in the strength given Him from God. . . . His life testifies that it is possible for us also to obey the law of God."

How then did Jesus live His life? He lived His life through dependence upon a power above Him, rather than depending upon the power within Him. This latter power would not have been sufficient. He lived through dependence upon divine power from His Father, in the same way that you and I can live by depending on the same divine power.

In John 5:30 Jesus says, "I can of mine own self do nothing." In John 14:10, He declared, I am in the Father and the Father in me. Even the words I speak unto you I speak not of Myself. And then He adds, The Father that dwells in Me, He does the works.

So Jesus' life was a life that was lived as a result of a faith or trust relationship with His Father. And He became a mighty demonstration and example of the fact that this same power is available to every one of us. Not even His miracles were performed by the power from within Him. His miracles were performed by faith and prayer (see *The Desire of Ages,* p. 536); they were performed by the power of God through the ministry of angels (see Acts 2:22; *The Desire of Ages,* p. 143). And the goodness we see demonstrated in His life, the perfect life of obedience, came from above Him rather than from within Him.

When we come to the close of His life, we find Him struggling in the Garden of Gethsemane. The weight that He had come to endure He had seen, all laid out before Him, when He was still in the heavenly country. But when we finally see Him sweating drops of blood there in Gethsemane, it looks as if He's not going to make it.

Some of us have had the idea that He was supposed to go through that all by Himself. That although all of His life He had been living through dependence upon His Father, now when He comes to Gethsemane and the cross, He has to do it alone. But Luke 22:43 says, right in the middle of the story, that an angel came and strengthened Him. How would you like to have been that angel? If you read the story in the inspired commentary, you'll find that it was the angel who took Lucifer's place, who came and encouraged Jesus and brought Him power to go through to the cross.

When Jesus was on the cross, He cried, "My God, my God, why hast thou forsaken me?" And we might say, That's it; now He's finally on His own. But not so. God Himself was in Christ, reconciling the world unto Himself. See 2 Corinthians 5:19. God and the angels were at the cross. See *The Desire of Ages,* p. 754. They were with Jesus right through to the very end. But Jesus didn't feel that they were. He *felt* as if He was forsaken.

And so all through His life, including His perfect, sinless behavior, including His miracles, including Gethsemane and the cross, Jesus lived through a power from above Him, and it was always through the faith relationship of prayer and communication with His Father that Jesus experienced this power. "Jesus revealed no qualities, exercised no powers, that men may not have through faith in Him. His perfect humanity is that which all His followers may possess, if they will be in subjection to God as He was."—*The Desire of Ages,* p. 664.

So, in the end, Jesus becomes our example. John 13:15 says it concerning the Communion service, but you can read quite a list of references to the point that Jesus was our example. Not even by a thought did Jesus yield to temptation. So it may be with us. See *The Desire of Ages,* p. 123. The sinless life that He lived was given us as our example. See page 49. By His own obedience to the law, Christ proved that through His grace the law could be perfectly obeyed by every son and daughter of Adam. See *Thoughts From the Mount of Blessing,* p. 49. Jesus' life in you will produce the same results as it produced in Him. See page 78. We are to overcome as Christ overcame. See Revelation 3:21; *The Desire of Ages,* p. 389.

Please, friend, don't let anyone tell you that we cannot obey the law of God. There's too much evidence contrary to that. And much of it comes from Jesus and the life that He lived, the teachings that He gave, and the example of His own life and how He lived it.

Now this brings us to a problem on which I would like to try to get down to the nitty-gritty. There seem to be three options concerning the nature of Christ. One is to believe that Jesus had an advantage over us, because He was like Adam before the fall. He could obey God's law. But we aren't like Adam; therefore, *we* can't obey the law of God. The second is to believe that Jesus was like Adam after the fall, and, therefore just like us. Because He could obey God's law, so can we. The third alternative is to believe that Jesus was like Adam before the fall, so far as sinlessness is concerned, but that He maintained that sinlessness by availing Himself of the same divine power that is available to us.

What is the weakness of the first option? For the person who defines sin in terms of the fallen nature, Jesus was like Adam before the fall. Therefore He was not a sinner by nature. But we are sinners. Therefore, Jesus was different from what we are. Because He was sinless, He can be our Saviour. So far so good. But we have difficulty with the next step: Because He was sinless, He cannot be our example.

The weakness of option number two is that, if Jesus was just like Adam after the fall, and, therefore, just like us, He might be able to be our example. But because He was a sinner He could not be our Saviour but would, instead, Himself need a Saviour.

But here is the third option: Jesus was like Adam before the fall in the sense that He was sinless, but He was like us in the sense that He inherited the temptations and weakness that we inherit. So, in one sense He had an advantage over us in that He began sinless. On the other hand, He had no advantage over us, that He had to depend on the same divine power to continue to overcome temptation that is available to us to overcome temptation. Viewed in this light He is both our Saviour and our example.

I believe that the third option is the correct one. I also believe that the issue in sin is far deeper than simply doing bad things. The issue in sin is basically the problem of a broken relationship—trying to live a life independent of God. In this sense, Jesus had far stronger temptations than we have, because, knowing that He was God, He had a much bigger temptation to live independently of His Father's power.

Jesus becomes more of an example to us if we consider sin in terms of relationship rather than simply of behavior. So the first two options are inadequate, and, if the third is correct—that the real issue is relationship and dependence—then whether Jesus had the nature of Adam before or after the fall becomes irrelevant to a large degree.

Now that I've finished telling you what I wanted to say, I'm going to tell you what I've said, with this brief synopsis.

The Nature of Christ

Jesus was God. As such He possessed the power of God *within* Him, including the power to lay down His life and take it again. The devil knew He had the power of God within Him and even tried to persuade Him to turn stones into bread. Jesus repeatedly spoke as God, yet He lived as a man because He was a man—"the man Christ Jesus." 1 Timothy 2:5. He became a man forever, accepting humanity after 4000 years of sin with its inroads on the human race, yet He ever has been and ever will be God.

Compared to Adam, Jesus was weak. He did not have the physical strength Adam had, He was not inherently as intelligent as Adam was, nor did He have the willpower that Adam possessed. Even though Jesus took on Himself these hereditary infirmities or weaknesses, He lived without sinning, doing always those things that pleased His Father. Not only did He not sin, but He was sinless. He loved righteousness and hated iniquity. He was tempted more than anyone who ever lived in this world, but He overcame sin and the devil in the same way that we can overcome. It is often asked, Didn't He have an advantage over us? Of course He did, because He was born God, whereas we aren't.

But He never used this advantage, because Jesus laid down the power of divinity within Him and lived His life as a man on this earth through the power of His Father from above Him. Even His mighty works were done through the power from above—by His connection with His Father, rather than through the power from within Him.

In summary: Jesus was divine as well as He was human. He took upon His sinless spiritual nature, our fallen human nature, in terms of physical strength, mental power, and moral backbone, after 4000 years of sin. In this weakened state, He gave us an example of victory from above rather than victory from within.

Obviously Jesus was different from us in some respect, but identical to us in others. What human being could claim to be God because God was his father? Not one of us could make such a claim. But Jesus could. In this respect He was different from us. But because He never used His divine powers on His own behalf, but depended for victory on His heavenly Father's power, as we must, He was in this respect the same as we are.

"The incarnation of Christ has ever been, and will ever remain a mystery. That which is revealed, is for us and for our children, but let every human being be warned from the ground of making Christ altogether human, such an one as ourselves; for it cannot be."—Ellen G. White Comments, *S.D.A. Bible Commentary,* vol. 5, p. 1129.

Another inexplicable point that we often waste endless hours in discussing is how Jesus could be in every way tempted like as we are. "It is a mystery that is left unexplained to mortals that Christ could be tempted in all points like as we are."—Pages 1128, 1129.

However, there are two major points that are important for us to remember concerning the nature of Christ. First He had no advantage over us in meeting sin and the devil. Second, he overcame sin and the devil in precisely the same way that we can overcome.

He may not have been subjected to every temptation that you and I encounter in life. But He was assailed with temptation on every principle on which we are tempted. He overcame by choosing from the very beginning of His earthly life to depend wholly on His heavenly Father's power to overcome, and it is our privilege to depend on our heavenly Father for the same overcoming power. Because He knew that as God in human flesh He possessed infinite power in His own right, His temptations must have been infinitely more severe than ours. And that's the real issue in the end anyway.

Each time I study this subject, I feel as if I'm on holy ground. To realize that Jesus came and lived as I have to live is an awesome thought. Does it make me feel as if I'm far behind? It sure does. Does it discourage me? No. Why? Because Jesus has given us too much evidence already that He loves us and will continue to help us to understand how He lived His life, so that we can too. We can take courage from that today.

(For additional references pertaining to this subject see *Countdown Desire,* pp. 199-203.)

Satan's original charge was that the law of God could not be obeyed. When man broke the law of God, Satan exulted and added another charge—that man could not be forgiven. He had no idea that God Himself would pay the penalty. But Jesus' life and death proved that sinners could be forgiven and that the law of God can be obeyed, not only by Jesus, but by those who live the life of faith as He did. This twofold message of forgiveness and obedience is the heart of the remnant's mission during the time of the three angels and the final work of Christ in heaven. Jesus as our High Priest provides forgiveness for sinners and power to obey. These two truths are equally necessary. It is extremely important that the remnant people understand this twofold work of Christ in heaven; otherwise, it will be impossible for them to fulfill their mission. Justification by faith (God's work for us) and the righteousness of Christ (which includes God's work in us) are the themes to be presented to a perishing world.

What Jesus Said About Sanctification

After a meeting one night in the Northwest, I was approached by a young man who said, "The gospel is that Christ died for our sins, according to the Scriptures."

And I replied, "Yes, that's good news, isn't it?"

But he continued. "That's *all* there is to the gospel."

"Isn't it good news that Jesus is coming again to take us to heaven?" I asked him.

"Yes, but it's not the gospel."

"Isn't it good news that Christ wants to come into our lives and live His life in us?"

"Yes, but it's not the gospel."

"Is it good news that there is power available for overcoming, for victory, for obedience, through the power of Christ?"

"Yes," he said, "but it's not the gospel."

"What does the word *gospel* mean?" I asked him.

"Well, er, uh, it means *good news!*"

Jesus had a lot to say about the gospel. He had a lot to say about the gospel of justification, of forgiveness, of His work for us. But He had at least twice as much to say about the gospel of sanctification, the work of Christ in us, in giving us power to live for Him.

We have all heard it said that Christ was our example, although there are some today who would question that, on the basis that we can never be exactly as Christ was. But if there was an area where Christ could be our example, where would it be? Have you ever thought about it? It could not be in the area of justification, for Christ never needed forgiveness, pardon, or reconciliation with God. But He *was* our example when it comes to living the Christian life. He was our example in obedience, in victory, in overcoming. Revelation 3:21 talks about it. So the subject of sanctification in terms of what Jesus had to say about it is so broad that we can only go over the highlights in this study. But if you are interested in knowing more about living the successful, victorious Christian life, you can find no better place to search than in the life and teachings of Jesus.

What did Jesus have to say about sanctification? Well, as such, we have just one text—John 17. He said that He wants His followers to be sanctified, the way He was sanctified.

But what is sanctification? To begin with we should notice that it includes several aspects in its modern understanding. First of all, it includes a finished work, something already done, and means simply to be set apart for a holy use. Second, we use the word to refer to living the Christian life, Christian growth, obedience, victory, power. We refer to it in terms of the work of the Holy Spirit *in* us. And I suppose we could even add a third aspect, that it is a completed work that God wants in His people who will live in His kingdom in heaven throughout eternity.

I'd like to begin with a description of sanctification and how it works, and then we will proceed with the biblical evidences.

Sanctification in Bible usage refers mostly to the completed work—being set apart for a holy use. The thief on the cross was both justified and sanctified. Obviously he had to have both a title to heaven and a fitness for heaven. Sanctification is also used in modern vocabulary to refer to Christian growth. But whether we are speaking of it as finished or ongoing, the method of sanctification is always by faith alone, just as much as in justification. Although we must think of justification and sanctification as separate with respect to acceptance and assurance, we must think of them together as to method of accomplishment in our experience.

This is not to deny that in sanctification both faith and works will exist. However, when we use the phrase sanctification *by* faith alone, we are making use of the usual understanding in the English language of the word *by*. (It refers to method. I travel to New York *by* plane. I make my living *by* working.) Every believer should understand that he is not merely to be saved by Christ's sacrifice, but that he is to make the life of Christ his own. The religion of Christ means more than the forgiveness of sin. It means taking away our sins.

How is this accomplished? Only by faith. The Bible truth is that those who have been justified by faith shall live by faith as well. Living the Christian life is accomplished through the same means by which the Christian life was begun. It is through faith only that we are able to keep God's commandments. Obedience by faith is the only kind of true obedience there is, and it is spontaneous, for the man of faith.

Obedience has to be by faith alone because of the nature of mankind. We are sinful by nature, and sinners are incapable of keeping the law of God apart from Christ. God wants to lead us to give up on ourselves and accept the righteousness of Christ for us, the righteousness of Christ worked out in us. Christ's righteousness for us is what gives us eternal life. Christ's righteousness in us is what produces genuine obedience and brings glory to God.

Everyone in the world is either controlled by God or controlled by Satan. See Romans 6:16. The only control we have is determining which of these two powers we want to control us. If we do not choose to enter into a continual relationship with God, the devil is in control of our direction and will ultimately be in complete control of us. This is called devil possession—the worst kind of slavery. If we choose to enter into a continual relationship with God, this enables God to be in control of our direction, and His Holy Spirit will ultimately possess us. This is the only real freedom there is.

Whenever we look away from ourselves and in our helplessness trust in total dependence on Jesus, this enables Him to dwell in us and to will and do according to His good pleasure. The result is that the righteousness of the law is fulfilled in us. This obedience is perfect obedience, but this does not mean that henceforth we are sinless. Unfortunately in our still sinful nature we do not live in uninterrupted dependance upon Jesus' power. For whatever reason, we take our eyes off Jesus. This is why we fall and fail. God is not to blame for this, but He has made provision for these lapses. The genuine Christian will remember that even though God has made provision for these failings, he must never make such provision an excuse for sinning. Making provision for sin is something for God to do, not us. Because the Christian is forgiven much, he loves much, and he that loves much, obeys much.

Obedience is the fruit of faith. This obviously settles the question of effort and cooperation in living the Christian life. We never deliberately work on result. Our *deliberate* efforts must be directed toward the *cause* of our obedience, not on the obedience itself. However, there will be many natural and spontaneous efforts that spring from the faith relationship. If without Jesus we can produce none of the fruits of righteousness, but through Him we can do all things, the only possible thing we can do in this whole business of salvation is to get with Him and stay with Him.

The deliberate warfare and striving spoken of in Scripture is always toward the faith relationship, not toward sin and obedience. Even resisting the devil is accomplished by submitting unto God and drawing nigh to Him. Those who believe in sanctification by faith plus works can only believe in imperfect obedience until Jesus comes. Those who believe in sanctification by faith alone can believe that perfect obedience has always been possible and is possible before Jesus comes.

Now I would like to give you the raw evidence, or at least a portion of it, for the conclusions I have just set forth.

There seems to be a great deal of emphasis nowadays that if we would just spend 90 percent of our time on the work that God has done for us, that this would be the proper emphasis. But in our study of the life and teachings of Jesus, we find in the inspired writings that the ratio is about one to four, with at least four times as much said about the work of God in us as is said concerning the work of God for us.

The foundation and walls of a structure are an analogy of what we are trying to say. As a result of this study, I have come to the conclusion that, while it is true that justification is the foundation of the gospel, sanctification is represented by the four walls built upon that foundation. There is much more emphasis upon sanctification than upon justification in the gospels, as well as in the instruction to this church through the gift of prophecy. I believe the explanation for this is as follows: The mission of the remnant people has been to build on the foundation of the Reformation. That's why we have so much information on this movement and are invited to build on it. And it is only as we do this that we will accomplish our mission. What is the world still waiting to hear? It is waiting to hear something that was supposed to have been built upon the Reformation theology of justification by faith—it is waiting to hear about the truth of sanctification by faith.

A growing segment of Christians want to believe that Jesus' living substitutes for my living. This is their philosophy: "I can't obey, so He obeyed for me when He was here on earth. His sanctification is in my place. He substitutes for me in sanctification." I've heard the text John 17:19 used as proof for this idea—"And for their sakes," said Jesus, "I sanctify myself, that they also might be sanctified through the truth."

I have searched for further light on this point, both in the Greek original and through commentaries, as well as through the inspired commentary to this church. The best help I found was in *My Life Today,* page 252: "Christ declared He sanctified Himself, that we also might be sanctified. He took upon Himself our nature, and became a faultless pattern for men. He made no mistake, that we also might become victors, and enter into His kingdom as overcomers. He prayed that we might be sanctified through the truth. What is truth? He declared, 'Thy word is truth.' His disciples were to be sanctified through obedience to the truth. He says, 'Neither pray I for these alone, but for them also which shall believe on Me through their word.' That prayer was for us; we have believed in the testimony of the disciples of Christ. He prays that His disciples may be one, even as He and the Father are one; and this unity of believers is to be as testimony to the world that He has sent us and that we bear the evidence of His grace.

"We are to be brought into a sacred nearness with the world's Redeemer. We are to be one with Christ as He is one with the Father. What a wonderful change the people of God experience in coming into unity with the Son of God! We are to have our tastes, inclinations, ambitions, and passions all subdued and brought into harmony with the mind and spirit of Christ. This is the very work that the Lord is willing to do for those who believe in Him. . . .

The spirit of Christ is to have a controlling influence over the life of His followers, so that they will speak and act like Jesus. . . .

"The grace of Christ is to work a wonderful transformation in the life and character of its receiver."—*My Life Today*, p. 252.

So when Jesus said, "I sanctified myself, that they also might be sanctified," He is our example, our pattern, in sanctification. We can be sanctified in the same way as He was—by dependance on divine power from above. It does not mean that He was merely sanctified in our place. Do you follow? He is our example and pattern in sanctification.

Well, then, let's proceed with what Jesus said about sanctification, with the subject subdivided into seven points. **Number one:** Method. What is the method by which sanctification is attained? It is by faith alone. In John 15:5, Jesus said, "Without me, ye can do nothing." Jesus is talking about producing the fruits of obedience and the fruits of the Spirit in the Christian life. If without Him we can do nothing, then it's all going to have to be done by faith in Him. In Mark 14:38, He said, "Watch ye and pray, lest ye enter into temptation." He gives us a clue as to how this is done. In John 6:28, the people had said, "What shall we do, that we might work the works of God?" Jesus replied, "This is the work of God, that ye believe on him whom he hath sent." Verse 29. And John 6:57, Jesus says, "He that eateth me, even he shall live by me." What does that mean? Verse 63 explains, "The words I speak unto you, they are spirit, and they are life."

So we have, through Christ's word, through prayer, through watchfulness concerning our relationship with Him, the methods for coming into dependence upon Him. In John 1:29, He said, through the lips of John the Baptist, "Behold the Lamb of God, which taketh away the sin of the world." This verse can be seen in two ways—first Behold the Lamb of God which taketh away the past sins; second, Behold the Lamb of God which taketh away our present sinning as well. It is only by beholding that we become changed. We are all aware of this truth. That principle works even in the world apart from Jesus. Whatever gets our attention gets us.

In Luke 10:42, in the story of Mary and Martha, Jesus said that there is only one thing needful, and that is to sit at the feet of Jesus and receive His grace through His Word and through prayer. In

Luke 16:13, Jesus said, in essence, that you cannot accept a gift and also earn it. That's one of the biggest questions facing us today. Can we ever earn or merit God's grace, whether it's in justification or sanctification? The answer is No! We can never earn or merit or work for God's pardon *or* His power.

There are two interesting texts that you might want to study that give a clear understanding of the fact that it is wrong to try to do that which only God has a right to do. John 10:33 is the first one. The Jewish leaders charged Jesus with blasphemy because He made Himself God by claiming to be one with His Father. If this had not been true, it would be blasphemy. And Matthew 26:51, 56 makes it quite clear that anyone who tries to save himself by his own efforts is in danger of forsaking Jesus.

So whether I'm trying to save myself by "being my own god," in justification, or whether I am trying to save myself in overcoming and obedience and victory, in sanctification, in the end I'm going to forsake Jesus. The reason for this is simple: Do-it-yourself salvation will not work. And if we take all of the three aspects of salvation—justification, sanctification, and glorification—and try to weave ourselves into any one of them, we are trying to save ourselves. In the end we'll forsake Him, just as the disciples did in the Garden of Gethsemane that night. On the other hand, it is blasphemy for a man to try to be God and try to save himself, regardless of which of the three aspects of salvation we are talking about.

When it comes to a faith relationship with Jesus, we're talking about the one thing we *can* and must do in response to God's offer of grace. This is more than just an intellectual assent to truth. It's something more than just hearing God's Word. That's why we ought to remember John 5:39, 40. There were people who did a great deal of searching of Scripture, but they missed the Saviour. The purpose of study and prayer is for communication, not just information. It's for communication and fellowship and relationship with God.

Number two: Genuine obedience and growth and victory are natural and spontaneous in the Christian life. We all agree that justification is the root and sanctification is the fruit. Now if sanctification is the fruit, let's not forget what Jesus told His disciples. He did not bid them labor to bear fruit. He invited them to put their effort toward abiding in Him. See *The Desire of Ages,* p. 677.

For the person who believes that sanctification is the fruit of the gospel, but who also believes that you are supposed to work hard on your own sanctification, there is a great incongruity. A tree doesn't labor to bear fruit. It bears fruit because this is its nature. Fruit is the result. One does not put forth effort on a result; he puts forth effort on the cause, and the result follows. Isn't that true? That's why the many statements that Jesus made concerning fruit are significant for this subject. Let's read just one of them, Matthew 7:17, 18. Let's start with verse 16 to get it in context: "Do men gather grapes of thorns, or figs of thistles? Even so, every good tree bringeth forth good fruit; but a corrupt tree bringeth forth evil fruit." Now notice: "A good tree cannot bring forth evil fruit, neither can a corrupt tree bring forth good fruit."

Ponder those words from Jesus. "A good tree cannot bring forth evil fruit." Genuine good fruit bearing is natural and spontaneous for a good tree.

Jesus said it again in Matthew 23:26: If you will wash the inside of a cup, the outside will be clean. How many of us have wasted our time and years and effort trying to clean up the outside of the cup, instead of going to the cause of the problem. If we put our attention on the cause and clean the inside, the outside *will* be clean.

In John 14:15-17, Jesus said in essence, If you love Me, you will obey. How many of us have wasted time and effort trying to obey, when Jesus said, If you love Me, you will! These are significant evidences from Jesus that genuine obedience is natural and spontaneous in the Christian life.

Then where is cooperation? *The Acts of the Apostles,* page 563, tells us that obedience is the fruit of faith and love. If that is true, then our efforts should be toward becoming good trees, by cooperating with God in coming to Him for the gift of the new birth, instead of toward trying to produce good fruit. (If you'd like to read further on this, there are two significant references: *The Desire of Ages,* page 668, and *The Acts of the Apostles,* pages 563-567.)

Number three: The essence of Jesus' teaching was self-surrender. See *The Desire of Ages,* p. 523. No one understands what

SANCTIFICATION 57

producing spontaneous fruit means until he has given up on himself. Perhaps that's one of the reasons why we have so much trouble with this question of whether obedience is natural or deliberate. It seems obvious that anyone who insists on deliberate obedience, forcing himself to obey, is one who hasn't yet surrendered himself. One who has to work hard on his performance is the one who hasn't yet given up on himself.

But one who has given up on himself and realizes that he can't succeed in his own strength, but depends on strength from above, is the one who begins to experience natural and spontaneous obedience. If self-surrender is the essence of Jesus' teachings, this makes genuine obedience a high priority. We have some mighty examples of self-surrender in many of Jesus' real-life parables.

You have the disciples who are sinking out on the sea. They didn't say, "God, help us." They said, "Lord, *save* us." A person who looks toward heaven and says, "God, I need some help," is actually admitting something. If I say to you, "I wish you'd come over and help me mow my lawn," and you, being in a friendly sort of mood, say, "Yes, I'll come over," you expect to *help* me.

So you come, and I say, "There's the lawn, and there's the mower. I'll be out back in the hammock." About that time your mood would change, and you'd probably say something like, "Wait a minute! You asked me to *help!*"

What do we mean by the word *help?* We mean, we'll do it together. You do part, I do part. When a person is going down for the last time, he doesn't say, "God, help me." He says, "Lord, save me." What does that mean? It means, "God, You're going to have to do it all."

When Peter was sinking, he said, "Lord, save me." Matthew 14:30. See also Matthew 8:25. The Bible also seems to have been referring to the matter of surrender in Luke 2:34, when it speaks about people falling and rising. They would have to fall and surrender before they could rise again. It's entirely possible that there are people who have been good church members all of their lives, but who will never be saved until they have a fall and realize how desperately they need to surrender to God and then let Him raise them up.

In Matthew 21 Jesus referred to Himself as being a stone. He said that the one who falls on this stone and is broken is the one who is ahead, rather than the one on whom the stone falls. No one understands genuine obedience of salvation in all of its entirety until he falls on the Rock and is broken. In Mark 9:43-48 Jesus said, If your arm or your eye offends you, pluck it out, cut it off. When you read the inspired help we have on that passage, in the book *Thoughts From the Mount of Blessing,* pages 60, 61, you discover that this is talking about self-surrender. Many people who are used to trying to working out their sanctification in their own strength but come to the realization that they must surrender to God and let Him work in them, talk as if it were almost like losing an arm or an eye. Self and their own works seem too precious to give up. But giving up on ourselves is precisely what Jesus taught was essential.

In Matthew 13:45, 46, Jesus talked about the pearl. You have to sell everything you have in order to buy the pearl of great price. The pearl includes salvation in all of its aspects. It reminds us that there is nothing more valuable than that. In Luke 14:33, Jesus said that one can't even be His disciple, unless he has given up on everything. It will cost everything.

And then, throughout the gospels, Jesus' references to the cross are significant. He speaks of death—death for us, as well as for Him. We must die, which means we must give up on ourselves, before we can understand genuine sanctification, obedience, victory, power, growth, and whatever else is included. If you want to study further on this, read *The Desire of Ages,* page 523, and *Christ's Object Lessons,* page 159. We cannot give up on ourselves; only God can bring us to that point. Even though we are the ones who give up, who surrender, it is only God who can bring us to the point of being willing to do so. Can you feature a person crucifying himself? It can't be done! It takes someone else to do the job. All we can do is to permit Christ to do it for us, and He will do it for us just as fast as we permit Him to.

Number four: The person who has given up on himself now has the privilege of accepting the two aspects of Christ's righteousness—Christ's righteousness *for* him and Christ's righteousness *in* him. There are those, unfortunately, who have given up and

SANCTIFICATION

accepted Christ's righteousness *for* them—justification—who have not given up and accepted Christ's righteousness *in* them—sanctification. It is actually possible to give up and accept Christ's righteousness *for* us without giving up and accepting Christ's righteousness *in* us. Such a surrender and acceptance results in one of the most subtle forms of salvation by works. Such persons think that, because they have been justified, their sinful works are acceptable to God.

Even though I believe that the cross and the finished work of Christ is enough to save me, if I haven't given up on the second aspect, in other words, if I continue to try to change my life, try to render acceptable obedience, try to work on victory, I am still a victim of salvation by works. The acceptance of Christ's righteousness in both aspects is a tremendous privilege. We must not miss out on it, or all is lost.

Christ's Object Lessons, page 67, tells us that the purpose of the Christian life is to reproduce the character of Christ in His followers. The purpose of the Christian life—but why? Is the purpose of the Christian life to produce His character so that we can be saved? No, it is to reproduce His character so that there can be honor and glory brought to God. Jesus made it clear in Matthew 5:16 that the fruits of righteousness are for glorifying God. John 15:8 declares that these fruits are for bringing glory to God. John 17:10 states that they are for God's glory. Luke 13:6 says that fruits are for God's glory. Our works, our sanctification, our obedience, our victories, are not for saving us in heaven; they are for bringing glory to God.

And if a person is interested only in getting to heaven and not interested in bringing glory to God, we might seriously question whether he can expect salvation in heaven. There is still bigger business than the certainty of our salvation—and that bigger business is to bring glory and honor to God.

Sanctification is the implanting of Christ's nature in humanity—Christ in the life. See *Christ's Object Lessons,* p. 384.

Number five: God's intention in His whole plan of salvation is to help us understand the privilege, the joy, the freedom of coming under His control. Jesus referred to this in Matthew 6:24, when

He said that no one can serve two masters. It's either one or the other. We are the servants of one master or the other; we are never in control of ourselves. The only control we have is to choose which master we want to control us. And in John 8:36, Jesus says that coming under His control will bring us freedom. "If the Son therefore shall make you free, ye shall be free indeed." John 8:36.

Study also the many references where Jesus talks about us as servants. A servant has a relationship to a master that is a unique relationship. The master is in charge. The master is in control. And even though Jesus called us His friends and we can experience that friendship because of the freedom that comes under His control, there is still the control of the Holy Spirit. Read it in *The Desire of Ages,* pages 258, 324, and 466, if you want further help on that. When we are under God's control, then God works in us to will and to do of His good pleasure.

Number six: As long as we are under the control of God, we can know the ultimate power of God. We don't have to wait until the end of our lives to get in one good day of knowing His power for obedience or victory or service. It is ours now—*so long as.* Take the disciples as a case in point. One day they cast out devils and come back rejoicing. The next time they try to cast out devils, it doesn't work. So they say to Jesus, "What's wrong? Why couldn't we cast them out?" On again, off again. What is the answer? It's a matter of "so long as." They were experiencing dependence upon God at one point and dependence upon themselves at another. Did that mean they were lost? No, they were still disciples. Jesus still loved them and kept walking with them. But they were still growing.

We see this in Peter's experience in Matthew 16. Jesus asked His disciples who people say that He is, and Peter replied, "You are the Christ, the Son of the living God." Yet, soon after this, Peter fell and failed miserably. Jesus had to rebuke him, saying, "Get thee behind me, Satan." But Peter was still Jesus' friend, and Jesus was still Peter's friend.

In John 11, Martha gave a beautiful exhibition of trust and dependence upon Jesus when He first arrived at their home after the death of Lazarus. But then, moments later, when Jesus asked

SANCTIFICATION

her to have the stone rolled away, she showed complete lack of trust.

In the growing Christian life, there are times when we are looking to Jesus, and we know the strength He has to offer. Yet there are also times when we are looking to ourselves, and we fall and fail. But so long as we look away from ourselves to Him, Satan has no power over us. Read it in *The Desire of Ages,* page 123, and *Steps to Christ,* page 62.

Number seven: Perhaps this is one of the most exciting of all—sanctification comes by justification. In Luke 7:43, Jesus said, "The more you are forgiven, the more you love." How can that be? What is the purpose for studying the Bible, for praying, for spending time every day strengthening one's devotional life with God? It is for the purpose of studying God's great love, His forgiveness, His grace. "It would be well to spend a thoughtful hour each day in contemplation of the life of Christ."—*The Desire of Ages,* p. 83. And by studying and contemplating and beholding His mighty love, His acceptance, His forgiveness, love awakens in our heart, and sanctification takes place. The more you love, the more you will obey. See John 14:15.

In John 8 the scribes and Pharisees dragged a woman to Jesus. Jesus said to her, "I don't condemn you." That's the cross. That's justification. "I don't condemn you." There is no one today who is condemned by Jesus, any more than the disciples were when they argued and bickered and fell. No one is condemned. Jesus did not come to condemn the world, but that the world through Him might be saved. See John 3:17. And it is only when we understand that aright that we can "go, and sin no more." Again, one is the result of the other.

We don't go and sin no more by trying hard not to—that's a dead-end street. The only way we can ever hope to go and sin no more is by discovering, and continually being reminded day by day, that God doesn't condemn us. And I'm thankful today for the good news that there is no condemnation for those who are in Christ Jesus. Are you thankful for that?

You know, it's not safe to talk about sanctification without having a good, clear picture of justification. Those who emphasize the truth of justification are emphasizing truth. If I don't have justification clearly in mind, I will think that sanctification is what my salvation is based on, and I'm going to get discouraged. We can stand today in the presence of God because of what Jesus has done. He does not condemn us. And we can be thankful for that.

But Jesus has also made provision for us to go and sin no more. And that is equally good news. There is power available to keep us from sinning, so long as we depend upon Him. "Oh," someone says, "I can't obey. I can't. I've tried." Neither could the paralytic walk. But Jesus said, "Rise, take up your bed and walk." And he did! See John 5:1-15.

"Oh," someone says, "I can't obey. It's impossible." Neither could Moses open the Red Sea. But he did!

Someone says, "I can't obey. Maybe someone else can, but not me." Joshua couldn't make the sun stand still—but through divine power he did!

Someone says, "I can't obey. It's too big an order." Neither could Gideon. Gideon couldn't wipe out the Midianites with 300 men and torches and trumpets. But he did!

Someone says, "I can't obey. The Bible might say it's possible. But I can't do it." Neither could Peter walk on water. But he did!

How are all of the imposssible things made possible? Notice what Jesus said: "With men this is impossible; but with God all things are possible." Matthew 19:26. He invites us to the realm of the impossible today.

(For additional references pertaining to this subject see *Countdown Desire,* pp. 204-216.

Satan's original charge was that the law of God could not be obeyed. When man broke the law of God, Satan exulted and added another charge–that man could not be forgiven. He had no idea that God Himself would pay the penalty. But Jesus' life and death proved that sinners could be forgiven and that the law of God can be obeyed, not only by Jesus, but by those who live the life of faith as He did. This twofold message of forgiveness and obedience is the heart of the remnant's mission during the time of the three angels and the final work of Christ in heaven. Jesus as our High Priest provides forgiveness for sinners and power to obey. These two truths are equally necessary. It is extremely important that the remnant people understand this twofold work of Christ in heaven; otherwise, it will be impossible for them to fulfill their mission. Justification by faith (God's work for us) and the righteousness of Christ (which includes God's work in us) are the themes to be presented to a perishing world.

What Jesus Said About Perfection

Perfection is a dangerous topic. To dwell very much on the subject of perfection can be a discouraging and defeating work, for invariably our attention is focused in on ourselves when we talk about perfection. And that's not where the power is—the power is always outside of ourselves. Therefore, when we deal with the question of perfection, it must be done lightly and once over, and be done with it.

We need to make a distinction right to begin with between *perfection* and *perfectionism*. Here is where we need a glossary—an explanation of the terms we are using. A person who is involved in perfectionism is one who becomes preoccupied with perfection. The perfectionist thinks of little else. He is the one who focuses his attention and everybody else's attention on it. The perfectionist is the one who insists that the sinful nature gets eradicated before Jesus comes, that not only can we overcome, but we can become sinless ourselves. I would like to disclaim any identity with perfectionism.

But the doctrine of perfection is a good Bible doctrine, a good Bible teaching, and Jesus had something to say about it. We could begin with Jesus' statements that He made to people on more than one occasion, "Go, and sin no more." See John 5:14; 8:11. That sounds rather unequivocal, doesn't it? We could deal with Jesus' statement in Matthew 28:20—"Teaching them to observe [or obey] *all* things whatsoever I have commanded you." That sounds rather complete. But there are three major passages that I would like to call your attention to briefly. The first is Matthew 5:48, the second is Matthew 22:11, and the third is Matthew 19:21-26.

Matthew 5:48. "Be ye therefore perfect, even as your Father which is in heaven is perfect." There are those who would like to say that the word *perfect* in the Bible means nothing more than mature. And it's true that the original Greek word includes the idea of maturity. And so, some say, it doesn't mean perfect—it means mature. But *mature* is a stronger word than *perfect,* for it carries with it the idea of ultimate perfection. Jesus allowed for stages of growth in the Christian life. This is clear in Mark 4:28: "First the blade, then the ear, after that the full corn in the ear." A blade is a perfect blade; an ear is a perfect ear. And the full corn in the ear is not only perfect, but mature as well. So we are told that at every stage of our development we may be perfect. See *Christ's Object Lessons,* p. 65.

This explains how you can have the word *perfect* attached to people like Abraham, Noah, Job, and others. They were perfect while they were still making mistakes and still failing. At every stage we can be perfect. But we are not ultimately perfect, or mature, until we come to the ultimate perfection that God has in mind. Let me explain.

You can have a newborn baby, and it can be a perfect baby that drools and coos. You can have a two-year-old who sits on the curb and goes blither, blither. And it can be a perfect two-year-old. But if someone is still doing that at age 20, we get a bit uneasy. If someone is still drooling and cooing at age 20, we know something is wrong. I'm thankful for this concept of growth, as given by Jesus, because it just may be that there are some of us still in the early stages of Christian growth!

When we study a text like Matthew 5:48, we can be thankful for the help that this church has been given. There are two major comments on this text that give important insights. The first is found in *The Desire of Ages,* page 311. Matthew 5:48 is quoted, then comes this statement: "This command is a promise. The plan of redemption contemplates our complete recovery from the power of Satan. Christ always separates the contrite soul from sin. He came to destroy the works of the devil, and He has made provision that the Holy Spirit shall be imparted to every repentant soul, to keep him from sinning.

"The tempter's agency is not to be accounted an excuse for one wrong act. Satan is jubilant when he hears the professed followers of Christ making excuses for their deformities of character. It is these excuses that lead to sin. There is no excuse for sinning. A holy temper, a Christlike life, is accessible to every repenting, believing child of God." So while we are growing in Christ, let's not make excuses for sinning.

One of the usual things that comes up when the idea of perfection is discussed is, "Have you [the person advocating it] achieved it? Has anyone, Christ excepted, achieved it?" These are foolish questions. We should never measure truth by our experience of it. That is a form of existentialism. If I go around saying that a thing is impossible because I don't know of anyone who has achieved it, I am taking a very naïve approach to the truth of God. There are many people who have reached God's ideal in the generations of this world. But they would be the last ones to know it or claim it, and those around them may not have had the capacity to recognize it fully either. But let's not say that it's impossible because of this.

The second major comment by Ellen White also quotes Matthew 5:48, and then says this: "The conditions of eternal life, under grace, are just what they were in Eden—perfect righteousness, harmony with God, perfect conformity to the principles of His law. . . . This standard is not one to which we cannot attain. In every command or injunction that God gives there is a promise, the most positive, underlying the command. God has made provision that we may become like Him, and He will accomplish this for all who do not interpose a perverse will and frustrate His grace."—*Thoughts From the Mount of Blessing,* p. 76.

In Christ dwells all the fullness of the Godhead. See Colossians 2:9. The life of Jesus is made manifest in our mortal flesh. See 2 Corinthians 4:11. That life in you will produce the same character and manifest the same works as it did in Him. Thus you will be in harmony with every precept of His law. Through love, the righteousness of the law will be fulfilled in us, who walk not after the flesh but after the Spirit. See Romans 8:4.

So if you're looking for help from the inspired commentary on the question of Matthew 5:48, note the following quotations.

Christ "has made provision that the Holy Spirit shall be imparted to every repentant soul, to keep him from sinning."—*The Desire of Ages,* p. 311. "Christ . . . proved [by His own obedience] that through His grace it [the law] could be perfectly obeyed by every son and daughter of Adam."—*Thoughts From the Mount of Blessing,* p. 49. "Perfect righteousness, harmony with God, perfect conformity to the law," this is the Bible "standard of character." This God "will accomplish" for us. See page 96. Jesus' "life in you will produce the same character" as was produced "in Him."—Page 78.

But this brings us to a problem. We have already noticed that it is the devil who says that we cannot obey perfectly. Then we come across a statement recorded in *Steps to Christ,* page 62, which says, "Because of his [Adam's] sin our natures are fallen and we cannot make ourselves righteous. Since we are sinful, unholy, we cannot perfectly obey the holy law." So the same author who says that this is the devil's charge apparently joins him in saying the same thing.

This raises the question of hermeneutics, the art of interpretation. How do we interpret Scripture? Here we need to be reminded of the historic Protestant method of interpreting Scripture. You take all of the inspired material you can find on the question, and you line it up, and you come to your conclusions based on the weight of evidence. Then you go back to the material that seems to be in conflict with your conclusions, and study it again to see if there is another understanding or explanation.

For example, Adventists believe from studying everything we can find on the condition of man in death that we are unconscious and in the grave until the resurrection. But there are one or two scriptures that don't seem to support that, for instance, the thief on the cross, and the parable of the rich man and Lazarus. So we came to our conclusion based on the weight of evidence; then we went back, looked at the hard texts, and discovered that they could be understood in a different way from what they first appeared.

Now we take the same principle and apply it to the question of whether or not man can obey God's law. I believe that you will find that, if you will study all of the evidence the Bible has on the subject, you will have to conclude God has made provision for us to perfectly obey His law.

So what do you do with *Steps to Christ,* page 62, and the few others statements like it? You go back and look at them again, just like we did with the question of the thief on the cross and the rich man and Lazarus. You discover another concept than that which you originally thought you saw there. I would like to invite you to take a second look at that passage in *Steps to Christ,* page 62, in its context. The context is discussing justification, not obedience and overcoming. It is saying that the law demands perfect righteousness in *all* of our past. Adam, before the fall, qualified. We do not. We will always have the burden of a sinful past, a bad track record, even if we were able never to sin again. Then it goes on to say, "More than this, Christ changes the heart." Then it goes on to explain that with Christ living in us, we are able to overcome and obey as He did.

Those of us who have studied this subject in the light of what Jesus had to say on it are confident that this conclusion is correct. We have no more uncertainty on this question.

The religion of Christ includes more than forgiveness. It includes setting us free form sin here and now. This doesn't mean that we will no longer be sinners. Even the apostle Paul acknowledged that he was the chief of sinners. He wasn't saying that he willfully continued to sin. He wasn't saying that apart from God, inherently in himself, he was still a sinner. Every true Christian will join him in that acknowledgment.

Now I'd like to ask the question, What is the purpose of perfection? Here is where we need to have it straight. We do not consider perfection as constituting the basis of our salvation at all. If we do, we will go straight into legalism, which leads either to discouragement or spiritual pride in denial that sin is sin. The purpose for whatever perfection God has in mind for His people is to bring honor and glory to Him. Those who obey God bring rewards for His suffering. See *Thoughts From the Mount of Blessing,* p. 89. Those who obey God and who by His grace experience perfection of character, honor Christ. See *Christ's Object Lessons,* p. 102. Those who obey God bring honor to Christ because the honor of God is involved in the perfection of the character of His people. See *The Desire of Ages,* p. 671. Christ put it this way, "Let your light so shine before men, that they may see your good works, and glorify your Father which is in heaven." Matthew 5:16. And the last group of God's people, before He comes again, "fear God, and give glory to him." See Revelation 14:7.

One of the dangers in dealing with this subject is that we get the impression that our perfection is what saves us. That is not so. Jesus and the cross is what saves us. Obedience and Christian perfection bring honor and glory to Him. But these are never something apart from God. He brings honor and glory to Himself through us. If it is Christ dwelling within, then it is His work. Are we going to exonerate God by our holy lives? No, God is going to exonerate Himself by whatever He can do in our lives. Let's never talk about it as if it were our own doing.

And once again, let us remember that no true Christian will ever go around claiming that he is perfect or sinless. That is a dangerous thing to do. The closer we come to Jesus, the more faulty we will appear in our own eyes. You can read an interesting comment on that in *Christ's Object Lessons,* page 160: "The nearer we come to Jesus and the more clearly we discern the purity of His character, the more clearly we shall discern the exceeding sinfulness of sin and the less we shall feel like exalting ourselves."

If you want to study something about how to be perfect and the need for perfection, study carefully Matthew 22. I would daresay that you will find more answers about perfection in that chapter about the wedding garment, coupled with the inspired commentary from *Christ's Object Lessons,* pages 312-319, than almost anyplace else you can turn. It is a fantastic passage from which to study this subject. We will go into Matthew 22 in the next chapter.

Now we turn to Matthew 19, the story of the young man who came to Jesus and wanted to know what he could do to enter into life. Jesus said, "Why callest thou me good? there is none good but one, that is, God." Verse 17. Then Jesus told him to keep the commandments. And the young man said, "I have kept all of these." Then in verse 21, Jesus said, "If thou wilt be perfect, go and sell that thou hast, and give to the poor, and thou shalt have treasure in heaven: and come and follow me."

I had a bit of a problem with that text for some time, because I

PERFECTION

wondered, How can a person be perfect, and *then* come and follow Jesus? This is an impossibility. You have to come to Jesus first, before you could ever hope to be perfect. But as you take a second look at this text, you'll discover that Jesus is actually telling us how to be perfect. There are deep spiritual lessons in this passage of Scripture. Go and sell all that you have. This is talking about more than just money. Get rid of what you have. You might be rich in talent. Stop depending on your talent. You might be rich in good looks—you're overcome every time you look in the mirror! Get rid of your dependance on your good looks. You might be rich in brains. Sell it, in terms of depending on it. Sell all that you have. Get rid of all the things that you depend on in any way as a substitute for dependance upon Jesus. Give up, not only on your money or talents or abilities, but on yourself. This is the essence of Jesus' teachings—self-surrender, giving up on self.

And then come and follow Jesus. Why was that added? Jesus said it in another passage, "Follow me, and I will make you fishers of men." Matthew 4:19. What is He talking about? He's talking about following Him in service. And no one can follow Him in service until he comes to the place of giving up on self-dependence.

Here is a classic statement from *The Desire of Ages,* page 641. "Those who minister to others will be ministered unto by the Chief Shepherd. They themselves will drink of the living water, and will be satisfied. They will not be longing for exciting amusements, or for some change in their lives. The great topic of interest will be, how to save souls that are ready to perish."

We'd better be sure we know what the gospel is before we try to tell it to someone else, that's true. But once we understand it clearly, then let's not sit around worrying about perfection, or looking for some change in our lives. Let's get involved in service to others.

We're never going to become perfect by dwelling upon perfection. It will come by dwelling upon Jesus. And the one who is involved in trying to help someone else know Jesus is the one who is going to be dwelling most upon Jesus Himself.

So let's get rid of everything that we depend on, whether it's in justification, sanctification, or glorification. Let's make Jesus our dependence. And just in case there is anyone who is discouraged as a result of these thoughts, let me ask you: Did Abraham in ignorance make missteps? Yes, he did. Did Elijah? Yes. Did Noah? Yes. Did the disciples? Yes. "If in our ignorance we make missteps, the Saviour does not forsake us. We need never feel that we are alone. Angels are our companions. The Comforter that Christ promised to send in His name abides with us. In the way that leads to the City of God there are no difficulties which those who trust in Him may not overcome. There are no dangers which they may not escape. There is not a sorrow, not a grievance, not a human weakness, for which He has not provided a remedy."—*The Ministry of Healing,* p. 249.

I am thankful today that although I am desperately in need of the grace of the Lord Jesus, and in my ignorance have made many missteps, that He has not left me, and He has not left you, friend. Please, let us not drag God's standard down to the level of our performance. Neither let us become discouraged, but keep our eyes on Jesus. And the work He has begun, He will complete. See Philippians 1:6.

(For additional references pertaining to this subject see *Countdown Desire,* pp. 216-220.)

Satan's original charge was that the law of God could not be obeyed. When man broke the law of God, Satan exulted and added another charge–that man could not be forgiven. He had no idea that God Himself would pay the penalty. But Jesus' life and death proved that sinners could be forgiven and that the law of God can be obeyed, not only by Jesus, but by those who live the life of faith as He did. This twofold message of forgiveness and obedience is the heart of the remnant's mission during the time of the three angels and the final work of Christ in heaven. Jesus as our High Priest provides forgiveness for sinners and power to obey. These two truths are equally necessary. It is extremely important that the remnant people understand this twofold work of Christ in heaven; otherwise, it will be impossible for them to fulfill their mission. Justification by faith (God's work for us) and the righteousness of Christ (which includes God's work in us) are the themes to be presented to a perishing world.

What Jesus Said About the Investigative Judgment

Jesus loved stories. He loved parables. In fact, most of the time He spoke in parables, and the Bible writers say He did not speak to the people unless it was parables. See Matthew 13:34. If Jesus were here today, perhaps He would be talking about electricity and airplanes and computers and all the rest of it.

One of His interesting parables is found in Matthew 22, His major parable regarding the investigative judgment. Many do not seem to realize it, but He referred to the investigative judgment on more than one occasion. His parable of the net as well as His parable of the wheat and tares imply a time of determination and decision-making *before* the final rewards are given. But perhaps His most detailed description of the pre-advent judgment is found in Matthew 22.

Many people have dreamed of being naked in public, but have you ever thought about going naked to a wedding? The probability is that most of us have not struggled too hard with that temptation. Streaking was rather short-lived, compared to other fads that have come and gone. It seems to me that streaking must have been terribly hard on the nervous system! But if the idea of going naked to a wedding sounds a little racy, consider this parable that Jesus told.

"And Jesus answered and spake unto them again by parables, and said, The kingdom of heaven is like unto a certain king, which made a marriage for his son." Verses 1, 2. Revelation 19:9, which tells us about the marriage of the King's Son, says "Blessed are they which are called unto the marriage supper of the Lamb." In the context of Revelation 19, you have the time predicted when Jesus gets together with His bride, the church, and the marriage takes place. So this parable refers to the last events just before Jesus comes again.

Back to Matthew 22: "And [he] sent forth his servants to call them that were bidden to the wedding: and they would not come. Again, he sent forth other servants, saying, tell them which are bidden, Behold, I have prepared my dinner: my oxen and my fatlings are killed, and all things are ready: come unto the marriage. But they made light of it, and went their ways, one to his farm, another to his merchandise: and the remnant took his servants, and entreated them spitefully, and slew them." Verses 3-6.

Here you have Jesus' reminder that although the Jewish people had built the tombs of the prophets, the prophets themselves had been roughly treated. Jesus was here giving a picture of the history of the nation that He was addressing. Some of the prophets who had taken the invitation to them had been persecuted and stoned and sawn asunder. Right down to the days of Jesus, the people had steadfastly rejected the invitation of God to come and be present at the wedding.

Verse 7. "But when the king heard thereof, he was wroth: and he sent forth his armies, and destroyed those murderers, and burned up their city." By this Jesus was evidently referring to the destruction of Jerusalem, in A.D. 70.

Verse 8. "Then saith he to his servants, The wedding is ready, but they which were bidden were not worthy. Go ye therefore into the highways, and as many as ye shall find, bid to the marriage. So those servants went out into the highways, and gathered together all as they found, both bad and good: and the wedding was furnished with guests." Here you have a picture of what took place shortly after Jesus' ascension, when the gospel was taken to the Gentiles. And this ingathering to the wedding feast continues all the way down to our day, isn't that true? We are a part of the people who are both bad and good.

Now when Jesus told this parable about the invitation to the wedding being taken to all, both bad and good, Jesus Himself knew that there's no one who is good. The apostle Paul nailed this down solidly in Romans 3 when he said, "There is none righteous, no, not one: . . . there is none that seeketh after God." Verses 10, 11. So how many righteous people are there? The Bible makes it clear that so far as we are concerned, we are bankrupt of righteousness. So what was Jesus saying here?

The invitation was to go to those who were bad, and who knew they were bad. But it was also to go to those who were bad, but who thought they were good! See Luke 18:9. On more than one occasion Jesus said, "They that are whole need not a physician; but they that are sick. I came not to call the righteous, but sinners to repentance." Luke 5:31, 32. When Jesus made this statement, He must have been referring to those who *think* they are good—people such as the Pharisees of His day. Jesus loved the Pharisees as well as He loves anyone else, and did His best to reach them. He loves the Pharisees of our day.

Notice here what it was that made a person worthy. It wasn't how good or how bad he was. The reason all those who persecuted the prophets and refused the invitation were not worthy was simply that they refused the invitation. That's what made them unworthy. Let's not think of worthiness in terms of behavior and performance, because that is not what makes us worthy. Worthiness is based on acceptance of the invitation.

And what is the invitation? In this parable we see God's justifying grace, provided at the cross, which made it possible for God to forgive sins. That's the invitation. Please notice that regardless of their outward performance, all, both bad and good, received the invitation to the wedding.

So now the wedding was furnished with guests.

In the days of Christ, it was customary for a wealthy person, a king in particular, when he put on a wedding, not only to send out an invitation, but to send the person invited a wedding garment to wear. That solved a lot of problems. Can you imagine receiving an invitation to the wedding of the Prince of Wales today? What would be the first thing the wife would say? You know what it is! "What am I going to wear?"

Back then, that problem was already solved. It made no difference whether you were rich or poor, whether your home was in a palace or in the ghetto. Anyone who received an invitation to the

78   WHAT JESUS SAID ABOUT

wedding also received a wedding garment. Even the poorest could look like a millionaire.

Kings went to a great deal of expense to provide wedding garments. So, if anyone were to show up at the wedding without the wedding garment on, it would be an insult to the king, to the king's son, and in a sense, to the whole kingdom.

So there were two things that came with a prominent wedding in the days of Jesus—an invitation and a beautiful robe to wear to the occasion. With that in mind, let's go on to verse 11.

"And when the king came to see the guests, he saw there a man which had not on a wedding garment." Evidently the king comes in to see the guests before the festivities begin, and when he comes in to investigate, to examine the guests, he sees there a man who isn't wearing the wedding garment.

Well, you may say, surely he had on his best suit or at least his jogging outfit. No, he was naked. Back to Revelation 3. The people who lack Christ's robe of righteousness are wretched and miserable and poor and blind and what? Naked! So I am going to go so far as to suggest that this man tried to "streak" to the wedding. And if you think that's going too far, about the most we could allow him, scripturally, is a few filthy rags, because all of our righteousness are as filthy rags. See Isaiah 4:6. Now I ask you, Which is better? Nakedness or filthy rags? They both sound pretty bad to me.

Can you see him there, shifting from foot to foot in front of the king? And the king is so kind. He treats him with dignity, which he really doesn't deserve. Verse 12. "And he saith unto him, Friend, how camest thou in hither not having a wedding garment? And he was speechless.". The king calls the man "friend." Isn't that good news? God is not interested in seeing how many people He can keep out of heaven; He's trying to see how many people He can get in. He asked, "Friend, how is it that you came without the wedding garment? Was there some misunderstanding? You must have received the invitation, because you're here. But what about the wedding garment? Didn't you get the package? Do you have some explanation you would like to make?"

He gives him a chance, doesn't he? But the Bible says that the man was speechless. He had nothing to say. Only then did the king say to his servants, "Bind him hand and foot, and take him

THE INVESTIGATIVE JUDGMENT 79

away, and cast him into outer darkness; there shall be weeping and gnashing of teeth. For many are called, but few are chosen." Verses 13, 14.

What is the wedding garment? Let's go back to Revelation 19 and the description of the marriage supper of the Lamb. "And I heard as it were the voice of a great multitude, and as the voice of many waters, and as the voice of mighty thunderings, saying, Alleluia: for the Lord God omnipotent reigneth. Let us be glad and rejoice, and give honour to him: for the marriage of the Lamb is come, and his wife hath made herself ready. And to her was granted that she should be arrayed in fine linen, clean and white: for the fine linen is the righteousness of the saints." Verses 6-8. Some of the modern translations say the fine linen is the righteous deeds of the saints.

What are the righteous deeds of the saints? What is the righteousness of the saints? Jeremiah 23:6 reminds us that the Lord is our righteousness. So any kind of righteousness that is seen in the saints is still the Lord's work, isn't it? Therefore, it isn't our righteousness; it's His righteousness. This story reminds you of the two aspects of Christ's righteousness that we are invited to understand and accept. First there is the righteousness of Christ for us at the cross, in providing the invitation. Second, there is the righteousness of Christ in us, worked out in the life through the power of the Holy Spirit and represented by the wedding garment. Both of them are of faith, and both come from Him.

As we look at these two aspects of righteousness in the parable Jesus told, we begin to see how these aspects apply today. The king came in to examine the guests. He saw there a man who was not wearing the wedding garment. Evidently the man wanted the invitation, he wanted to be at the wedding, but he either neglected or rejected the wedding garment.

"Of those who accepted the invitation, there are some who thought only of benefiting themselves. They came to share in the provision of the feast, but had no desire to honor the king."— *Christ's Object Lessons,* p. 309. (Read pages 307 to 319.) Let's paraphrase the quotation. It is talking of those whose only interest is in getting themselves to heaven, while at the same time having no desire to accept Christ's righteousness lived out in the life for the purpose of bringing honor to Him. David put it this way, "He leadeth me in the paths of righteousness for *his* name's sake." Psalm 23:30. Emphasis supplied.

I'd like to remind you that if your primary purpose for being a Christian is to get yourself to heaven, you may never be there. There is bigger business than our own salvation, and that bigger business is bringing honor and glory to the King and His Son.

"By the wedding garment in the parable is represented the pure, spotless character which Christ's true followers will possess."—*Christ's Object Lessons,* p. 310. "This robe, woven in the loom of heaven, has in it not one thread of human devising."—Page 311. Please notice that. Sanctification, Christ living His life out in me through the Holy Spirit—obedience and victory and overcoming—have in them not one thread of human devising. All we can do is accept them as gifts. "By His [Jesus'] perfect obedience He has made it possible for every human being to obey God's commandments. When we submit ourselves to Christ, the heart is united with His heart, the will is merged in His will, the mind becomes one with His mind, the thoughts are brought into captivity to Him; we live His life. This is what it means to be clothed with the garments of His righteousness."—Page 312.

So when the king comes in to view the guests, in this preadvent judgment, he sees the man without the wedding garment, and he asks, "Friend, why?" There are at least two things that the King examines in this investigative judgment. First, He examines to see whether or not the invitation has been accepted—and continues to be accepted. Second He sees whether or not the wedding garment has been put on. Jesus said in Matthew 24:13 that he who endures to the end, the same shall be saved. It is not enough to once accept the invitation; the invitation must be accepted continually. And in addition to that, the robe must be put on. Revelation 3:5 uses the same imagery: "He that overcometh, the same shall be clothed in white raiment, and I will not blot out his name out of the book of life, but I will confess his name before my Father, and before his angels." Not only does God want us to have the invitation to the heavenly country, but He also wants us to be overcomers, by His grace, as well. And that's what putting on the garment is all about.

So when God comes in to examine or investigate the guests, He comes to *reveal* before the universe those who have not only accepted the invitation, and continued to accept it, but also to see whether those who have accepted the invitation have put on the wedding garment and become overcomers through His power as well.

Someone says, "Wait a minute, preacher. You're going into the things that I'm afraid of. You're going into the things for which people are changing their theology today. You're taking away my assurance and certainty when you talk to me about overcoming, because I'm not doing too well on that."

But I'd like to remind you that if overcoming were my work, then there would be good reason for me to be nervous too. In fact, there would be nothing but hopelessness. But the truth is that overcoming is Jesus' work, and that truth has evaded us. Many of us have missed that truth.

There have been voices that have insisted that our justification is by faith alone, and we've had some real rocking of the ship on that point. But perhaps we needed to take a long look at that. One of the problems of the church, going way back, is that we early took the cross and justification for granted. Let's give priority to the invitation, because of the cross. It's free, even though it's not cheap. It's free for all, both bad and good. But you cannot, if you are going to be honest with Scripture, deny that there is a robe, and the robe has to do with overcoming and with the righteousness of Christ *in* the life.

The man in the parable, when asked about the robe, was speechless. He had nothing to say. And only then was he dismissed from the marriage. Notice that the reason he had nothing to say was because he knew he could have had the robe on. Nobody will ever be speechless in the judgment unless they have had a clear understanding about the robe and have turned it down. I think there's heavy truth there. God never holds us accountable for truth that we didn't have or understand. (Read these chapters: John 9; 5; Romans 1.) With that understanding, we realize that this man must have understood how to receive the robe, but he neglected to put it on, or he turned it down. He had no excuse. Then, and only then, was he shown to the exit. It wasn't putting on the robe that took him to the marriage. And it isn't our obedience that saves us in heaven. But it just so happens that when a person accepts the invitation, God wants him to also accept the robe that comes with the invitation. We should never try to separate them.

Perhaps a little illustration would help. When I was at Pacific Union College, the college hired professors to teach there on the basis of their expertise, their training, their degrees, their studies. They invited them to join the faculty on that basis. But every professor who comes to teach at PUC had to take a TB test, because it just so happened that the board and faculty there didn't want any teacher going around the campus coughing and sneezing TB germs on everyone else. The TB test had nothing to do with the basis on which someone was invited to teach at the college, but passing the TB test remained a *condition* for teaching there.

Now the invitation that Jesus gives to everyone to come to the marriage of the Lamb is based totally on what Jesus has done, and what Jesus has done is enough. That is the basis of the invitation. But it just so happens that God doesn't want people coughing and sneezing sin germs all over His universe. And so He has made putting on the robe a *condition* for entrance into heaven.

Does that help? Maybe it doesn't. Perhaps you say, Regardless of how it is explained, it still comes down to the same thing. There goes my assurance. Even though you call one a basis, and the other simply a condition, if it's true that I can go to the marriage because the invitation if free, but I'll be thrown out if I don't have on the robe, then I might as well forget the invitation too, because I don't feel that I have the robe on yet.

Well, here's another explanation. Suppose I came to you and said, "I have a brand-new Cadillac Seville that I want to give you, and the down payment is free. I'm giving you a Cadillac Seville with no down payment." What would be one of your first questions? "How much are the monthly payments?" Right?

OK, the monthly payments are $1000 a month for the next 10 years. Are you interested?

You would probably say, "Forget the Cadillac Seville. What value is it to have no down payment if the monthly payments are going to finish me off? That's a pretty expensive gift!"

THE INVESTIGATIVE JUDGMENT 83

Now suppose the Lord Jesus Christ comes to you and says, "I have made provision at the cross to give a free invitation to the marriage supper of the Lamb."

And you say, "Thank God. Marvelous grace! What's the rest of it?"

"Well, you have to have on a robe at the wedding that is perfect, and you have to weave the robe yourself."

You know what I would say at that point? I would say, "You can forget the invitation, because there is no way I can accomplish that. The only option I have is to walk away from the invitation."

But there is one thing that we have missed. Seventh-day Adventists have missed it. The Christian world has missed it. (Once in a while we berate ourselves for not having finished the work of God. Well, I'd like to give you some cheap comfort. Nobody else has finished it either!)

We're all in the same boat on this one. And I want to propose that the truth of what I am going to say next is truth that is part and parcel of the three angels' message and the latter rain. It is this: The wedding garment is just as free as the invitation. Did you catch that? THE WEDDING GARMENT IS JUST AS FREE AS THE INVITATION! We've missed that. If the wedding garment was something I had to produce myself, and it had to be perfect, then I would have to say when the invitation came, "Forget it. I'm not going to the wedding at all." But the wedding garment is free. It's a gift. That's why the man was speechless.

What are we saying by that? We're saying that sanctification is just as much a gift as is forgiveness. Overcoming is just as much a gift as is pardon. It's not something you achieve; it's something you receive. This truth has been trying to come to the surface for some time now. And if you think we've had ebb and flow over the question of justification, just stand by for the ebb and flow over this one. It's a big one. Because many people who are willing to accept God's grace in terms of the invitation will refuse the wedding garment. Why? Because they want to weave themselves into the work. They want to weave their own garment!

That's why the strong people in the church are the ones threatened by the total message of the righteousness of Christ. That's why we have strong people, self-disciplined people, who say,

"Yes, we can only enter heaven on the basis of the cross, but when it comes to living the Christian life, you've got to work hard at it. You've got to do your part, and let God do what you can't do. You've got to use your willpower, your determination, your backbone to try to obey, try to overcome, try to get victory."

I wish I could say it fifty times in fifty different ways. The robe is as free as the invitation! The reason we have not overcome and the reason we make excuses for our sins and the reason we have to get rid of the judgment, perfection, the gift of prophecy, and all the rest of it, is that we have not seen this point—the robe is as free as the invitation.

Now how that works out in real life needs to be explained. Here's a little story that may illustrate what I'm trying to say. It's the story of Charlie.

Charlie sat in the back row in a class I was teaching in California. Now at the back of the room, the row went all the way across, with an aisle up the middle to the back row. And Charlie sat in that middle seat in the back row.

Charlie was a little older than the other students, and I also decided after the first day or so that he had gotten into the class by mistake, because he kept staring at me. I didn't like the way he looked at me at all. I got the feeling he didn't like me very well. He spoiled the class for me. Every time I looked at him I would lose my train of thought. So, I would teach the kids on one side for a while, and then I would talk over Charlie's head to the kids on the other side. Then I'd go underneath, and back over to the first side again. But I didn't want to meet Charlie's eyes.

The class Charlie was taking was called the dynamics of Christian living. We talked a lot about righteousness by faith in that class. At the end of class one day, Charlie stayed behind and asked, "Teach, can I talk to you?"

I said, "Yes." So we went to my office, and we sat down. I said, "What do you need?"

He said, "I don't get it."

"You don't get what?"

"I don't get this business of righteousness by faith."

And I thought to myself, "If you'd listen, instead of staring at me all the time, you might get it!" But I said, "Well, Charlie, tell me a little bit about yourself."

And he began to tell me a most fascinating story—an unbelievable story. It had only been three or four months before that time that Charlie had been sitting in jail, waiting trial for murder. One day his mother came in. She was dying of cancer. She tried to talk to him through the bars, but all she could do was weep, and as she cried, Charlie began to cry. She said Good-bye, and that's the last he ever saw her alive.

He went back to his cell, and he cried for three days. At the end of the three days, he looked up toward heaven and said, "If there is a God up there, I could sure use You."

His case came up in court. To everyone's surprise all the charges against Charlie were dropped, and he walked down the streets of the city a free man.

He went to the home of the girlfriend he had been living with for the past couple of years. She was overjoyed to see him, but at the same time he arrived she was having a Bible study with a Christian Bible worker in the living room. She invited Charlie to stay for the Bible study, but he said, "Oh no. No!" And he went into the back room and waited until it was over. After the Bible worker left, he came out of the back room, and began to talk to her about continuing their relationship where they had left off. She was no longer willing to do that, but she promised to find him a place to live. So she found him a place and talked him into coming to the Bible study the next week.

Well, he continued to listen to the Bible studies, and then there were some public meetings there in the San Francisco Bay area, and he went to the meetings. He was touched by the story of Jesus and how Jesus had taken his place and died for his sins. Charlie gave his heart to the Lord during those meetings. Later Charlie was baptized, giving a public confession of his acceptance of Jesus Christ as his personal Saviour. He became a Seventh-day Adventist.

But he still had a problem. In fact, he had four of them. He was still drinking, he was still cussing, he was still smoking, and he was still on drugs. And somewhere along the line he had gotten the idea that these were not too good! He tried hard to quit, but the harder he tried, the worse he got.

Have you ever discovered that it is possible to fight the devil so hard you almost become like him? It is possible to look at yourself so long in the mirror that you begin looking more like yourself. Charlie's attention was focused on himself, and although he kept trying and trying to overcome these things, he just couldn't do it. After several weeks of desperate effort, he looked up toward the same God that he had looked up to in the prison, and he said, "God, if anything gets done about these problems, You're going to have to do it, and You're going to have to do it ALL."

Oh! By that time I was sitting on the edge of my seat! I asked, "What happened?"

"Well," he said, "when I got to the place where I prayed that prayer, God came in to my life, and He took away my desire for all four of them. They were gone."

I said, "Really?"

"Yes."

"What happened then?"

Then the Bible worker and his girlfriend said to him, "Why don't you go to college and make something of yourself?"

He told them he couldn't go to college, because he hadn't even gone to high school. But they insisted. They said, "You can take a GED test, and only one person in a hundred flunks a GED test, and you can go to college." So he took the GED test, and he flunked it. He was one in a hundred!

So he came to Pacific Union College, where I was teaching at that time, and he applied for admission. At that time the college was turning away 300 students a year that they didn't have room for. And in spite of the flunked GED test, they accepted him. Another miracle!

I said to Charlie, "How are you doing?"

"Well," he said, "English is my hardest subject. I'm getting A's in English. But I just don't understand this business of righteousness by faith!"

And right there I wanted to laugh! I said, "Hold on, Charlie. Righteousness by faith is more than a theory. It's an experience. And it sounds to me like the Lord has given it to you."

Then I asked him, "Would you mind telling a little bit about this to the class tomorrow? I think they would like to hear what Jesus has done for you."

"Oh," he said, "do you think I should?"

And I said, "Yes."

"Well," he said, "if you think I should, I will." And I did, and he did. But the interesting thing was that, when he told his story to the class the next day, I noticed something that I couldn't miss. Charlie talked more about Jesus than he did about Charlie. And that is proof of someone who has really turned his life over to Jesus, isn't it?

But the story made me angry in one way. When I thought of all the years that I had tried to get the kind of victories that God had *given* to Charlie, it made me angry. But then I began to realize whom I was angry at. I wasn't angry at God. God doesn't treat people differently. He wasn't unwilling to do for me that which He was willing to do for Charlie. God is not a respecter of persons. So what was the difference? The problem was that all the time I had been trying to *win* what had been *given* to Charlie. That was my problem. The robe is a gift. It is just as free as the invitation. If that weren't true, there'd be no hope for any one of us, because we cannot produce one bit of righteousness ourselves; it must all come from Christ. And I believe with all my heart that at any time, anywhere, a person gets to the point of helplessness that Charlie reached, he receives the same gift that Charlie received.

Have you accepted the invitation to be present at the marriage supper of the Lamb? If you have accepted Jesus as your personal Saviour and accepted that Christ died for your sins according to the Scriptures, then you've accepted the invitation.

Have you accepted the robe, the wedding garment? That gets a little heavier, doesn't it? So many of us are painfully aware that we fall and fail and sin. But obedience is just as much a gift as is pardon and justification. Overcoming sin is not something we work hard at to accomplish; it is a gift from God. The wedding garment is free—just as free as the invitation. It is yours *so long as* you accept it. And it is accepted through the continuing relationship with Christ, who will lead you to accept it more and more constantly.

As you see Him day by day and attempt to learn in experience as well as in theory what it means to receive both the invitation and the robe of His righteousness, may I invite you to RSVP. The King invites you to the marriage supper of the Lamb. Will this be your reply?

"To the King of kings and Lord of lords. I received Your Majesty's pressing invitation to be present at the marriage supper of Your Son, Jesus. I pray Thee, let me be excused."

Or will you say this?

"To the King of kings and Lord of lords. I have just received Your Majesty's urgent invitation to be present at the marriage supper of Your only-begotten Son. I hasten to reply. By your grace, I'll be there. P.S. And thank You for the beautiful robe."

Investigative Judgment

DA 104.1	Judgment teaching brings sense of need
DA 107.1	Standing before God decided by character and life (DA 239.2)
DA 113.1, 2	Jesus is our representative
Matt. 21:12-15	Cleansing the temple—type of judgment (DA 158.1)
DA 173.5	If you don't understand the sanctuary you don't understand the judgment
John 5:22, 27	Jesus given full right to judge
John 5:24	Believers not judged (NEB, RV) (DA 210.4)
John 5:43-45	Who accuses us in the judgment
Matt. 12:41, 42	Judged by Nineveh and Queen of Sheba
DA 314.1	The only one who can judge is the one who knows motives
Matt. 13:30	Judgment at the time of the harvest
COL 122.2	The gospel gathers both bad and good—the judgment separates them
COL 127.3	The mediatorial work of Christ
Luke 12:2	Whatever is covered up will be uncovered
Luke 12:8, 9	Confess Christ and He confesses us
Luke 12:11, 12	When brought to "judgment" don't have to worry about defending yourself
Luke 12:57-59	Sinner should settle with his "opponent" before the judgment
COL 212.1	Judgment and mercy
COL 227.2	The gospel includes the pre-advent judgment
Luke 16:1-9	COL 372.2 Even the unjust steward prepared for the judgment!
DA 507.1	Jesus ascended to complete the work begun on earth
COL 165.1	Judgment for the sake of God's people
COL 166.3	Satan's accusing work
COL 166.2	Judgment to avenge us of our adversary
COL 166-170	Read all! (Zech. 3:1-3)
Mark 11:13	The time of the figs was not yet (Gentiles) DA 583.1; 1 Peter 4:17; 7BC 979
Mark 11:13, 14	Close examination whether fruit or not **before** sentence
Matt. 22:11	The king looks at the guests—judgment! (COL 310.1)
DA 736.7	Light shed on what the Judge is like

Satan's original charge was that the law of God could not be obeyed. When man broke the law of God, Satan exulted and added another charge–that man could not be forgiven. He had no idea that God Himself would pay the penalty. But Jesus' life and death proved that sinners could be forgiven and that the law of God can be obeyed, not only by Jesus, but by those who live the life of faith as He did. This twofold message of forgiveness and obedience is the heart of the remnant's mission during the time of the three angels and the final work of Christ in heaven. Jesus as our High Priest provides forgiveness for sinners and power to obey. These two truths are equally necessary. It is extremely important that the remnant people understand this twofold work of Christ in heaven; otherwise, it will be impossible for them to fulfill their mission. Justification by faith (God's work for us) and the righteousness of Christ (which includes God's work in us) are the themes to be presented to a perishing world.

What Jesus Said About Prophets

Jesus stood silent. He did not speak—not even a word. In spite of the many questions put to Him, in spite of desperate attempts to induce Him to speak, He remained silent. It was the most solemn response Jesus ever made, and there is significant truth to be learned today from that silence.

It was during His trial before Herod. Jesus had been arrested in Gethsemane. He was taken to the court of Annas, then to Caiaphas, and then before the Sanhedrin. He had been brought to Pilate, and Pilate, in turn, sent Him to Herod. "And when Herod saw Jesus, he was exceeding glad: for he was desirous to see him for a long season, because he had heard many things of him; and he hoped to have seen some miracle done by him. Then he questioned with him in many words; but he answered him nothing." Luke 23: 8, 9.

When I first read about Jesus' silent treatment of Herod, I was happy. Herod was the one who had killed John the Baptist as a result of a drunken party with his lords and his rash oath to Salome. So when I read how Jesus treated him, my reaction was "Good for You, Lord! That's the way. Show him whom he's been fighting against. Ignore him. Be rude." And if I had been in Jesus' shoes, I would have curled my lip and put a scowl on my face; I would have looked daggers at Herod. But then I realized that Jesus didn't feel that way at all. Jesus came to this world to die for Herod as much as He came to die for me.

We shouldn't see Jesus' silence as being rude and vindictive toward Herod. Instead we should see Him standing there silently, perhaps with tears in His eyes, sorrowing that another one of His created children had turned Him down. Jesus was simply accepting the decision that Herod had already made. Herod had rejected the message of John the Baptist, the greatest of the prophets, and there was nothing more that even Jesus Himself could do or say to reach him.

John the Baptist was a prophet and "more than a prophet." Matthew 11:9. Yet he taught the people that Christ was greater than he. See Luke 3:16. He was a lesser light to lead them to the Greater Light. He was the Lord's messenger. See Matthew 11:10. Have you ever heard of anyone in modern times who was more than a prophet, who was a lesser light leading to the Greater Light, and who was called the Lord's messenger?

There has been a modern counterpart of John the Baptist, a "more than a prophet," and there was a record of once before when a prophet had been "more than a prophet." We find that record in Number 12. Miriam and Aaron had decided that Moses was nothing special. They said, "Hath the Lord indeed spoken only by Moses? hath he not spoken also by us?" Verse 2. God Himself came to Moses' defense, appearing in the pillar of cloud at the door of the tabernacle. He explained to Miriam and Aaron that Moses was indeed more than a prophet, and then He asked, "Wherefore then were ye not afraid to speak against my servant Moses?" Verse 8. Miriam, who had been foremost in the criticism, was stricken with leprosy.

Herod, who should have been afraid even to speak against the Lord's messenger, was so insensible of John's importance in the eyes of heaven that he put him to death! And when the voice of the prophet was silenced, Jesus Himself had nothing more to say. He had nothing to say because it would have been useless to say more. From the story of Jesus and Herod we can learn that if one is unfriendly to the prophets, he is going to be unfriendly to Jesus Himself. The two attitudes always go together.

One of the outstanding characteristics of the people in Palestine at the time of Christ's first advent was that they had problems with the prophets. They had always had problems with the prophets. In the days of Christ they came along and garnished the tombs of the prophets and said, "If we had lived in the days of our fathers, we would not have treated these wonderful prophets the way they did." They splashed on the whitewash and hung the wreaths. And then they went back to Jerusalem, after their buckets were empty, and planned to put Jesus to death!

Jesus spoke hard-hitting words to them: "Wherefore ye be witnesses unto yourselves, that ye are the children of them which killed the prophets. Fill ye up then the measure of your fathers. Ye serpents, ye generations of vipers, how can ye escape the damnation of hell?" Matthew 23:31-33.

The apostle Paul had something to say on this point too: "For they that dwell at Jerusalem, and their rulers, because they knew him [Jesus] not, nor yet the voices of the prophets which are read every Sabbath day, they have fulfilled them in condemning him." Acts 13:27. So Paul made it clear that whatever the people did to the prophets, they did to Jesus, and their relationship to the prophets was simply a prelude of how they would relate to Jesus.

In Acts 7 we find the well-known experience of Stephen, sometimes called the first Christian martyr. In the middle of his final discourse, he broke off from his review of the history of Israel and ringingly accused his listeners: "Ye stiffnecked and uncircumcised in heart and ears, ye do always resist the Holy Ghost: as your fathers did, so do ye. Which of the prophets have not your fathers persecuted? and they have slain them which shewed before the coming of the Just One; of whom ye have now been the betrayers and murderers: who have received the law by the disposition of angels, and have not kept it." Verses 51-53.

This was too much for his hearers, and they rushed at Stephen, dragged him out of the city, and while a young man named Saul collected the coats, they stoned him to death. But in his last moments of life Stephen saw a vision. He looked up into heaven and saw Jesus at the right hand of God, *standing up*. I've always liked that part of the story. Jesus was not going to take this attack on His servant sitting down. He was standing up for Stephen. And Stephen died in peace, praying for his enemies. He had spoken the truth. And it went too deep; it hurt too much. He had said, "You people listen to the prophets every Sabbath and pay lip service to the prophets, but you reject them and the One of whom they spoke." The same can still be true today.

In the parable of the rich man and Lazarus, Jesus told how the rich man asked that Lazarus be allowed to return from the dead to warn his five brothers. But Jesus had Abraham tell the rich man, "If they hear not Moses and the prophets, neither will they be persuaded, though one rose from the dead." Luke 16:31.

Shortly after Jesus gave this parable, another Lazarus *was* raised from the dead, proving Jesus to be correct, for even the resurrection of Lazarus from the dead did not convince those who rejected the instruction and warnings given by the prophets. And when Jesus Himself was raised from the dead, those who, along with Herod, had refused the testimony of the prophets and put Him to death were filled with terror. But still they were not persuaded.

Jesus always manifested the utmost regard for the prophets. "Think not that I am come to destroy the law, or the prophets," He said in Matthew 5:17. At another time He promised that "he that receiveth a prophet in the name of a prophet shall receive a prophet's reward." Matthew 10:41. The gospel writers point repeatedly to events in His life, saying, "This was done, that it might be fulfilled which was spoken of the Lord by the prophet." Matthew 1:22; 21:4. See also Matthew 2:15; 3:3; 8:17; Luke 3:4; John 1:23; 12:38. Early in His ministry Jesus read from the book of the prophet Isaiah in His own hometown church on the Sabbath day. As a result He was ushered outside and pushed to the edge of a nearby cliff. See Luke 4:16-30. He quoted from or alluded to the prophets repeatedly in His teachings—from Daniel (Matthew 24:15), from Jonah (Matthew 12:39), from Moses (Luke 24:27), and others.

Jesus spoke to the Jewish leaders, warning them of the danger of following man-made traditions instead of the commandments of God. See Matthew 15:1-9. And His disciples, forgetting how often He had read minds, came to Him and said, "Knowest thou that the Pharisees were offended, after they heard this saying?" Verse 12. Jesus responded by giving one of His shortest parables: "Let them alone: they be blind leaders of the blind. And if the blind lead the blind, both shall fall into the ditch." Verse 14.

This short parable is relevant today; for the church called Laodicea, the last church until just shortly before Jesus comes, also has, among other things, a problem with blindness. See Revelation 3:14-22. So it was not only the people in Christ's day who were blind!

The apostle Paul, comparing the different parts of the body to the different parts of the church, speaks of the eyes of the church. See 1 Corinthians 12. Now, eyes are for seeing, and in 1 Samuel 9:9 we discover that in Bible times a prophet was sometimes called a "seer"—a see-er, or one who sees. In giving to His remnant church the gift of the prophets, God has provided eyes so that we who are members of the remnant church can take heed to the prophetic messages and escape being either blind followers or blind leaders. The people in Christ's time, blind as they were, had no reason to be blind, for "eyes" had been provided for them. They were blind because they refused to see. See Matthew 13:14, 15. Seeing, they did not see, and hearing, they did not hear. Jesus said to them, "If ye were blind, ye should have no sin: but now ye say, We see; therefore your sin remaineth." John 9:41. It was in rejecting the light that was available to them through the seers that they became blind, and that very rejection of light made further enlightenment impossible for them.

Jesus Himself spoke of the impossibility of reaching those who reject the prophets. In His farewell to Jerusalem, He cried out, "O Jerusalem, Jerusalem, thou that killest the prophets, and stonest them which are sent unto thee, how often would I have gathered thy children together, even as a hen gathereth her chickens under her wings, and ye would not!" Matthew 23:37.

On the afternoon of the resurrection, as Christ was walking toward the little village of Emmaus, He was endeavoring to bring encouragement to two men. Their hearts were heavy, their eyes, filled with tears. They recalled for this Stranger the events of the past few days. And with all of the resources of heaven at His command, Jesus chose one method above all others to reach their minds and comfort their hearts. "And beginning at Moses and all the prophets, he expounded unto them in all the scriptures the things concerning himself." Luke 24:27. Jesus designed that His people should be guided by the messages given through the prophets. It was for this reason that He gave the prophets top priority by His own teaching and example.

On the basis of Jesus' teachings, on the basis of Scripture, and on the basis of the repetition of history, I submit that whatever you do with the prophets, you will sooner or later do with Jesus. If you accept the prophets, listen to them, and follow their counsel, you will accept Jesus and listen to Him and follow Him. If you reject the prophets and ignore their messages, you will reject and ignore the Lord Jesus. The people of Israel were not unique in their problems with the prophets, and we are invited to learn from their experience. "All these things happened unto them for ensamples: and they are written for our admonition, upon whom the ends of the world are come." 1 Corinthians 10:11.

Within our church today, the experience of the Jewish people is being repeated. *The Desire of Ages,* page 235, describes it this way: "The Jews misinterpreted and misapplied the word of God, and they knew not the time of their visitation. The years of the ministry of Christ and His apostles,—the *precious last years of grace to the chosen people,—they spent in plotting the destruction of the Lord's messengers."* Emphasis supplied.

The story is told of a man who went to an exhibit of some famous artwork. As he was viewing some of the paintings, he remarked to his companion, "They say this stuff sells for millions of dollars. Why I wouldn't give you a nickel for the whole lot of it."

A guard was standing nearby. Hearing the man's comment, he stepped over to him, tapped him on the shoulder, and said, "Sir, these paintings are not on trial. But those who view them are."

The lesson is true today. "Many a man who delights to quibble, to criticize, seeking for something to question in the word of God, thinks that he is thereby giving evidence of independence of thought, and mental acuteness. He supposes that he is sitting in judgment on the Bible, when in truth he is judging himself. He makes it manifest that he is incapable of appreciating truths that originate in heaven, and that compass eternity. In the presence of the great mountain of God's righteousness, his spirit is not awed. He busies himself with hunting for sticks and straws, and in this betrays a narrow and earthly nature, a heart that is fast losing its capacity to appreciate God."—*The Desire of Ages,* p. 468.

God's gift of prophecy, whether in the Bible or in the inspired gift to the church, is not on trial today. It has been tested and proved. *We* are the ones who are on trial. It rests with us what the outcome of our trial shall be, whether we will accept of His gift or whether we will be in Herod's shoes and receive no other message from heaven. Those who reject the voice of Jesus through His prophets will find in the silence of Jesus the most solemn rebuke that mankind can receive. "Wherefore then were ye not afraid to speak against my servant?"

The Prophets

DA 31.2	The prophets had ceased (GC chapter 1)
DA 32.4	When we depart from God, the prophets are uncomprehended
DA 59.3	Prophets among the heathen
DA 65.5	Wrong motive for searching the prophecies—to exalt self
DA 101.2	Prophet needed to prepare people for Christ
DA 101.3	The prophet John had no formal education
John 1:21	"Are you Elijah?" "No, I am not." (See Matt. 11:14; 17:10-13; Luke 1:17; Mal. 4:5, 6.)
DA 103.4	John did not fully understand (DA 220.2; 136.4; 216.2, 6; 276.4)
DA 103.4	John's understanding developed
DA 105.2	Faking acceptance of the prophet for greater influence
John 3:26-30	People uplift the prophet, the prophet uplifts Jesus (DA 108.2)
Matt. 4:6	The devil quotes the prophets out of context (DA 124.1)
DA 133.3	Long time since Israel had a prophet
DA 139.2	Jesus' teaching illuminated the prophets
DA 167.2	Those who reject the prophets don't prosper
DA 188.1	Prophets' role to settle controversy
DA 193.1	Jews misinterpreted the prophets—caused the Samaritans to go "sola scriptura"
John 5:46, 47	If you don't believe the prophet you won't believe Jesus
DA 317.2, 3	Disregard the prophet and you will disregard Jesus
Luke 7:26, 27	John—more than a prophet
Matt. 11:14	"John is Elijah"
Luke 11:34-36	The light of the body is the eye! (See 1 Cor. 12:17, 21, 25, 28. Compare 1 Sam. 9:9.)
MB 93.1	How light can become darkness
MB 2.0	Misinterpreting prophecy for selfish reasons
Matt. 5:12	Prophets persecuted
MB 33:2	Negative publicity is *still* publicity!
Matt. 5:17	Jesus didn't come to destroy the prophets
DA 234.1	Christ spoke through *all* the prophets
DA 235.2	Plotting the destruction of the prophets
DA 468.2	Judging the Bible is judging yourself
MB 54.1	The prophet points out the self-centered
MB 55.2	Christ's truths had been taught by the prophets
Luke 6:39	The blind need eyes (the seer—1 Sam. 9:9)
Matt. 7:15	Beware of false prophets (MB 145.2)
Mark 4:9	COL 39.1 Why inspiration is rejected! (COL 41.4)

WHAT JESUS SAID ABOUT

Luke 8:16-18	Don't cover up light!
COL 127.4	New truth *glorifies* the old truths (COL 128.0)
Matt. 10:41	Reward by receiving the prophet
Matt. 15:14	If you have no eyes (prophet) then you are blind
DA 396.3	Satan distracts from real issues by minor questions
DA 407.2	If you don't hear the prophets, no miracle will benefit you
DA 425.2	Heaven verified what the prophets had said
John 9:29	The Pharisees believed in "sola scriptura"
Luke 10:16	The downward path of rejecting truth (DA 490.0)
DA 494.3	A clearer understanding than the prophets had of their own writings
Luke 11:47-53	Reject one and you will reject all
Luke 13:28	Prophets in the kingdom and you thrust out
Luke 13:34, 35	Result of killing the prophets—left desolate
Luke 16:31	If you don't listen to the prophets you won't listen to Christ
Luke 18:31	Everything the prophets wrote will come true
DA 567.1	Jesus—more than a prophet
DA 584.3	To reject prophet of your day is to reject the prophets since the beginning
DA 587.5	Israel hated the prophets because they revealed their secret sin
COL 278 2, 3	Why John's message as a prophet was rejected
COL 293.1, 2	The way you treat the prophets is the way you'll treat the Son (DA 596.3)
Matt. 23:30	"If we had lived in the time of our ancestors"—DA 618.2
Matt. 23:30-37	Those who kill the prophets
DA 618.3	The more the light, the more serious the rejection of that light
John 13:19	"I tell you before it happens so that . . ."
DA 667.1	Prophecies literally fulfilled
DA 730.4	No further word for one who rejected the prophet (Luke 23:9; DA 731.3)
Luke 24:27	Beginning with Moses and the prophets (DA 799.0, 2)
Luke 24:44	Everything came true

Satan's original charge was that the law of God could not be obeyed. When man broke the law of God, Satan exulted and added another charge—that man could not be forgiven. He had no idea that God Himself would pay the penalty. But Jesus' life and death proved that sinners could be forgiven and that the law of God can be obeyed, not only by Jesus, but by those who live the life of faith as He did. This twofold message of forgiveness and obedience is the heart of the remnant's mission during the time of the three angels and the final work of Christ in heaven. Jesus as our High Priest provides forgiveness for sinners and power to obey. These two truths are equally necessary. It is extremely important that the remnant people understand this twofold work of Christ in heaven; otherwise, it will be impossible for them to fulfill their mission. Justification by faith (God's work for us) and the righteousness of Christ (which includes God's work in us) are the themes to be presented to a perishing world.

What Jesus Said About Devil Possession

The choir had just finished singing the morning's anthem. With a soft rustle of robes, the singers returned to their places in the choir loft and sat down. A slight stir ran through the congregation as people shifted in their seats, seeking the most comfortable position to sit out the sermon. The church was crowded that morning, and suppressed excitement was in the air, for the morning speaker had a reputation for being controversial. He wasn't often invited to express His views publicly, and rumors had it that one such service had actually ended in a near riot. The platform elder was understandably a bit nervous as he glanced toward the guest Speaker and nodded slightly to indicate that the time had come for Him to begin.

The speaker had scarcely reached the podium and opened His mouth to speak when the doors to the rear of the sanctuary crashed open. Shrieking and staggering up the center aisle, a demoniac hurled himself into the presence of Jesus. You can read about it in Luke 4:33-36. "In the synagogue there was a man, which had a spirit of an unclean devil, and cried out with a loud voice."

The description is a bit humorous—"an *unclean* devil." After all, how many *clean* devils are there? But at least we can assume that as devils go, this particular devil was a bad one. This demoniac "cried out with a loud voice, saying, Let us alone; what have we to do with thee, thou Jesus of Nazareth? art thou come to destroy us? I know thee who thou art; the Holy One of God." Verses 33, 34.

Notice the pronouns—they are very interesting. "Let *us* alone." "What have *we* to do with thee?" "Art thou come to destroy *us?*" Evidently the demon began by speaking both for himself and for the man that he possessed. But then he ended with "*I* know thee." Perhaps the man did not fully realize in whose presence he had been so violently placed. But the demon certainly recognized whom he was confronting.

This must have been a rather nervy demon. Perhaps he felt especially adventurous that day when he decided to interrupt the church service where Jesus—the One who had created him—was holding forth. But nervy or not, he also must not have been particularly smart. He should have known better, because he ended up defeated—as the demons always do in the presence of Jesus. For "Jesus rebuked him, saying, Hold thy peace, and come out of him. And when the devil had thrown him in the midst, he came out of him, and hurt him not. And they were all amazed, and spake among themselves, saying, What a word is this! for with authority and power he commandeth the unclean spirits, and they come out." Verses 35, 36.

In the Bible are seven recorded instances when Jesus confronted demons. Before we consider the second occasion, please notice three things: (1) Jesus' contact and conversation with the demon was brief, (2) the demon was forced to leave his victim immediately, and, at least in this particular case, (3) there was no intermediary present. In other words, no one was involved in bringing the afflicted man to Jesus or in seeking Jesus' help in his behalf. He came alone. In fact, the man wasn't even capable of asking help for himself, for when he tried to speak, the demon spoke through him. Yet Jesus was still able to deliver and save him. These are pertinent questions for today among those who have studied this question of spiritual warfare.

The second case history, Matthew 9:32-34, is very short: "As they went out, behold, they broguht to him a dumb man possessed with a devil. And when the devil was cast out, the dumb spake: and the multitudes marvelled, saying, It was never so seen in Israel." In this case, there were intermediaries, for the Bible says that "*they* brought to him a dumb man possessed with a devil." Once again, however, the encounter was brief. And the evidence is that the demons were forced to leave immediately at Jesus' word.

The people who brought this man to Jesus couldn't do anything to help him. But they knew enough to bring him to Jesus, and that's the right thing to do, wouldn't you agree? Anyone today who knows someone who is tormented or oppressed or in trouble because of a devil should follow the example of these people in bringing that one to Jesus. He is the only One who has the power to bring healing and restoration.

At the time of this confrontation, the Pharisees dropped a seed of doubt. Notice verse 34: "The Pharisees said, He casteth out devils through the prince of the devils." This seed was to germinate and grow and do its ugly work in the minds of the people. We'll hear more about it later. But the Pharisees always did their best to discredit Jesus.

Case history number three is found in Matthew 12. "Then was brought unto him one possessed with a devil, blind and dumb: and he healed him, insomuch that the blind and dumb both spake and saw." Verse 22.

The record continues with a dialogue between Jesus and the Pharisees. But Jesus' actual encounter with the demons again was brief and again ended in their total defeat. This time also there was an intermediary—the man was brought to Jesus. The religious leaders continued to enlarge upon their accusation that Jesus cast out devils by the power of the devil. In return, Jesus gave them some hard-to-answer arguments and told a parable about an empty house—swept and garnished—where seven demons returned to take the place of one that had been expelled. We'll come back to this, but for now let's continue with the fourth case history.

It is found in Matthew 8:28. "And when he was come to the other side [of Galilee] into the country of the Gergesenes, there met him two possessed with devils, coming out of the tombs, exceeding fierce, so that no man might pass that way." Jesus and His disciples had made their way up from the shore and were met by these men, blood dripping from where they had cut themselves, matted beards, glaring eyes, frothing and screaming and naked. Their cries could be heard all around the countryside.

The disciples beat a hasty retreat back to their boats, but Jesus remained behind. When the disciples slowed down and looked around sheepishly, they saw Jesus was right where they had left Him—His upraised hand holding the demons at bay. Demons are always helpless and powerless in the presence of Jesus. And you can see the disciples slowly returning, one by one, making sure to stay behind Jesus—where it was safe!

In this instance, Jesus engaged in a brief dialogue with the demons. According to Luke 8, He asked, "What is your name?" And their spokesman replied, "My name is Legion." In the days of Christ, the Roman army was made up of legions. Each legion consisted of from three to five thousand men. Apparently the devil has enough spare demons that he can waste three to five thousand of them on one or two men.

Modern exorcism apparently uses this example of exorcism as the basis for its practice of conversing with demons. The modern popular approach says that you have to talk to each individual demon and coax them out one by one.

Inspired counsel to God's last-day church warns regarding spiritualism in the last days, just before Jesus comes again. The Seventh-day Adventist Church has taken a strong stand against attending spiritualistic séances. Why? Because in the spiritualistic séance, even though it may appear that a person is talking to their dead relatives, they are actually talking to impersonating demons.

And yet, under guise of spiritual warfare and modern exorcism, there are Seventh-day Adventist Christians who are sitting up half the night speaking directly to demons. How subtle are the devil's deceptions!

Although there *is* Bible evidence for multiple possession, there is no authorization for Christ's followers to deal individually with each demon. When Jesus gave the command, *all* the demons left. A package deal, if you please. In the case of the Gadarenes the devils went into the swine, the swine ran into the sea, and the people came out and pleaded for Jesus to leave their country before they lost any more of their resources.

In this case there was no intermediary. Once again the demons exhibited a lack of judgment by coming into the presence of Jesus voluntarily. They were perceptive enough to say, as recorded in

Matthew 8:31, "*If* thou cast us out, suffer us to go away into the herd of swine." Emphasis supplied. They surely must have known what the outcome of the encounter was going to be! If they had been wise, they would have stayed back among the tombs. Then again, perhaps they *were* smart enough to know what would happen, but too weak-willed to resist trying to show off!

This is the only occasion in Jesus' ministry when the demons were named. They said their name was Legion. Apparently it was referring only to their number—it had nothing to do with their function or work. Apparently all 3000 to 5000 of them went under the same name! It was the name of their group, or company.

There is a concept in the modern spiritual warfare that has become popular today that each demon has a name, indicating his work. And so in a case of multiple possession, it is necessary to cast out the temper devil, and the lust devil, and the hay-fever devil. I have heard of people being exorcised of the rock-'n'-roll devil and the clumsiness devil. But there is no biblical support to be found for this practice.

The fifth case history is found in Matthew 15:21-28. This is the story of the Syrophoenician woman whose faith was so great. She persisted, staying in Jesus' presence to catch some of the crumbs from the Master's table. She saw such compassion in Jesus' face that even the abrupt words He spoke for the benefit of His disciples could not obscure His love. Her problem was that her daughter was grievously vexed with a devil. At the conclusion of the conversation, Jesus said, "O woman, great is thy faith: be it unto thee even as thou wilt." Verse 28. Matthew concludes his account of this miracle by saying, "And her daughter was made whole from that very hour."

There was an intercessor in this account, but the daughter who was possessed wasn't even present. She received deliverance in absentia, we might say. And even though she was not in His immediate presence, she was delivered immediately at His word.

Case history number six is found in Mark 9:14-29. This is a long one. Jesus comes down from the mount of transfiguration with Peter, James, and John. He had taken three of His disciples on a special trip. The other nine felt jealous because they hadn't been invited and had been bickering among themselves about who was to be the greatest, when a man brought his demon-possessed son to be healed. Still nursing their feelings of jealousy, they tried to take on the demons, but instead, the demons thwarted their efforts. Although Jesus never lost a case, His disciples did. This was just the kind of case the religious leaders had been waiting for. If Jesus' disciples couldn't handle this particular demon, maybe Jesus couldn't either.

When Jesus arrived, He was drawn into a conversation with the boy's father. After explaining the desperate condition of his son, the lad's father said, *"If* you can do anything—" Jesus replied, "All things are possible to him who believes." Then the man answered, "I believe, but evidently I don't believe enough. Please help me with my unbelief." See Verses 22-24. And Jesus healed the boy. There was a great deliverance that day.

In this case the father was the intermediary. It appears that the boy's healing was contingent upon his parent's faith. When Jesus rebuked the demons, they left. There was no argument or long, drawn-out discussion.

After the crowds had melted away, the disciples asked Jesus why they hadn't been able to cast out this demon themselves. And Jesus said, "This kind can come forth by nothing, but by prayer and fasting." Verse 29. But Jesus, who cast the demon out, hadn't been fasting, so far as we know. It's easy to take a literal interpretation of this and think that somehow God in heaven will look down and say, "If these people will go without eating for a period of time and beg Me to help them, I will be impressed and will move in their behalf." No, not at all. This doesn't line up with what Jesus said about God being *willing* to give good gifts to His children. You don't earn power over the demons by going without eating, by doing penance, by effort, or by struggling. So what did Jesus mean?

The prayer and fasting that Jesus had been involved in included a continuing relationship with His Father. He didn't try to rein Himself up into some kind of spiritual high just for this occasion. Rather, He spent time every day in communion and fellowship with His Father. He was thus kept in His Father's control and was ready for whatever devices of the devil He might be called upon to face at a moment's notice.

On the other hand, His disciples had not spent the night or the early morning in fellowship with heaven as He had. While Jesus had prayed and communed with His Father, they had fallen asleep while arguing and fighting and scrapping about who was to be the greatest. *The Desire of Ages,* page 431, says this: "The selection of the three disciples to accompany Jesus to the mountain had excited the jealousy of the nine. Instead of strengthening their faith by prayer and meditation on the words of Christ, they had been dwelling on their discouragements and personal grievances. In this state of darkness they had undertaken the conflict with Satan." By their own choice they had separated themselves from the power of heaven and were thus left to meet the enemy in their own feeble strength.

If at any time we try to grapple with the powers of darkness on our own, we will surely be overcome. Unless we have the power of Jesus, it is sheer folly to attempt a confrontation with the devil. He is stronger than we are, and he will come out on top in the end, even if he lets it appear that we won. Only the power of Jesus is strong enough truly to overcome the enemy, and this power is available to each of us through a daily relationship with Him. Not only are we incapable of dealing with devil possession in its most extreme form, but we are also incapable of dealing with the devil's temptations and tricks in our daily lives. We cannot overcome sin in our own strength. We can overcome only through the strength of heaven as we come to Jesus and allow Him to fight for us. There we can find rest and peace.

Finally, case history number seven. Here we don't have a story, as we do in the other instances. We have only a reference to something that had already happened. Mark 16:9 says, "Now when Jesus was risen early the first day of the week, he appeared to Mary Magdalene, out of whom he had cast seven devils." Now I suppose we could speculate on this, as to whether Jesus cast out seven devils all at once or cast devils out of Mary seven different times.

In *The Desire of Ages,* page 568, we read, "Seven times she had heard His rebuke of the demons that controlled her heart and mind." And in the parable Jesus told in Matthew 12, it is explained how a person who has been once freed from demon control can again be devil possessed. Let us read verses 43 to 45. "When the unclean spirit is gone out of a man, he walketh through dry places, seeking rest, and findeth none. Then he saith, I will return into my house from whence I came out; and when he is come, he findeth it empty, swept, and garnished. Then goeth he, and taketh with himself seven other spirits more wicked than himself, and they enter in and dwell there: and the last state of that man is worse than the first. Even so shall it be also unto this wicked generation."

What does Jesus mean by this? He is suggesting that there's something more important than merely getting the devil cast out. It is also necessary to *keep* him out. Isn't that true? And Mary had to learn that—evidently the hard way.

A person may know a mighty deliverance from sin—even from devil possession—but unless he has a vital connection with God— a continuing fellowship with Him day by day through Bible study and prayer—it's not going to be enough. Sin is never stamped out by us. It is crowded out as Jesus comes in. No wonder that when Mary learned this, she could never be pulled away from Jesus' feet. She learned what it meant to sit at Jesus' feet and hear His word, and that's what kept the demons from returning.

Have you ever wondered how a person becomes devil possessed in the first place? If you analyze these biblical case histories, you conclude that devil possession doesn't happen overnight. Unless a person deliberately places himself on the devil's ground by choosing to delve into the occult, devil possession generally is the end result of a long process.

However, anyone who chooses to live a life apart from God day by day is under Satan's control, and his direction is downward. The devil may win one, lose one, win one, lose one. But he continues to push downward until the person is his completely— until he has absolute control over that person all of the time. We call this devil possession. But there is a more sophisticated form of devil possession, such as was exhibited by the religious leaders of Christ's day. They didn't froth at the mouth or wallow in the dust or scream obscenities. But they were even more hopelessly possessed than the demoniacs, because they didn't see their need for deliverance and therefore didn't come to Jesus. See *The De-*

sire of Ages, p. 256. It is interesting to note that while Jesus was able to cast the demons out of those who were demoniacs, He never even attempted to exorcise the demons that controlled the Jewish leaders, even though they were possessed by the same evil spirits. Yet the devil came to dominate them so completely that he worked through them to crucify Jesus.

The process of coming under Satan's complete control can be reversed. If a person keeps seeking to know God, day by day, and knows what it means to sit with Mary at Jesus' feet in fellowship and communion, God takes control of his direction—and his direction will be up. Even though a growing Christian experiences ups and downs, even though God too will win some and lose some, God's goal for the committed Christian is ultimately to have total possession and control of him all of the time. We could call this being possessed by the Holy Spirit. Does that sound good to you? It sounds good to me. And I believe it is God's goal for every person.

But Jesus had compassion for those who had gone the other direction. He brought deliverance to them, and it is still good news today that He has the power to cast out demons. He told His followers, "Heal the sick, cleanse the lepers, raise the dead, cast out devils." Matthew 10:8.

We can draw several conclusions from our study of these case histories.

1. When Jesus casts out devils, He casts them out immediately. No long period of sweating it out or praying it through or getting involved in long dialogues with the demons. When Jesus moves in on the devils, they've had it. And if that is not also true in our confrontations today, I would like to suggest, based on Scripture, that perhaps the devil is playing games with us because of our lack of the power of Jesus. And if we don't have the power of Jesus, we'd better not try to tangle with the demons.

2. Jesus cast out all of the demons at once, not one at a time. Jesus never cast out demons piecemeal. We see no evidence for that, although the case of Mary Magdalene suggests that those who have been delivered at one time can be possessed again if they neglect to continue inviting God to control their life.

3. When it comes to intermediaries, sometimes there were

intermediaries, and sometimes there were not. On the basis of Scripture, we cannot conclude that it is essential to have an intermediary, or, as some have termed it, an intercessor. It happened both ways in Jesus' time.

4. Casting out devils is no big deal! The last thing in the world a Christian should want to be known for is his ability as an exorcist. In Luke 10:17, when the seventy returned and said, "Lord, even the devils are subject unto us through thy name," Jesus replied in essence, "*So?* Satan was cast out of heaven a long time ago. He's a defeated enemy."

Could it be that the devil is thrilled when we become preoccupied with him and decide that every little thing that comes along is some sort of devil harrassment—and we focus our attention on him and try to dialogue with him and find out all of his names? There is no basis in Scripture for such a practice. What we do find in Scripture is the assurance that Jesus' power is greater than all the hosts of darkness.

Some Christians think and speak altogether too much about the power of Satan. They think of their adversary, they pray about him, they talk about him; and he looms up greater in their imagination. True, Satan is a powerful being; but, thank God, we have a mighty Saviour who cast out the evil one from heaven. Satan is pleased when we magnify his power. Instead, why not talk of Jesus? Why not magnify His power and His love? (See *The Desire of Ages,* p. 493.)

The way Jesus treated the demon possessed is good news. It was good news in Palestine, and it is good news today. Jesus never lost a case. The devils screamed for mercy in His presence. Therefore they are nothing to be afraid of, for the mighty name of Jesus is still the greatest power on earth. God has not given His people "the spirit of fear, but of power, and of love, and of a *sound mind."* 2 Timothy 1:7. Emphasis supplied.

If Jesus, in His love and compassion, was able to deliver the poor demoniacs in every case, He ought to be able to do something for you and me today, don't you suppose?

One of these days the world, the flesh, and the devil will be no more because of what Jesus has done. When He was here, He gave proof in miniature of that which He had the power to do ultimately. The death of Jesus effectively and forever dealt the deathblow to the enemy. May each of us know what it means today to be controlled by the Holy Spirit and to be excited about the good news of the freedom Jesus still offers.

Devil Possession

DA 36.3	Stamp of demons on men's faces—possessed with legions of evil
DA 38.0	Christ came to expel demons that control the will
Matt. 8:16	Jesus drove out the evil spirits with a word (TEV)
Matt. 8:28-33	The demoniacs at Gadara (Mark 5:1-20; Luke 8:26-39; DA 337-341)
Matt. 9:32-34	Man who couldn't talk because he was possessed by a demon
DA 116:4	Never does one leave the ranks of evil for God's service without encountering the assaults of Satan
Matt. 10:1, 8	Disciples given power to drive out evil spirits (Mark 6:7-13; 3:13-15) (DA 490—look on devil as defeated foe)
Matt. 11:18	John the Baptist accused of having a demon
Matt. 12:22	Man blind and dumb because of demon's control
Matt. 12:24	Pharisees' charge: Jesus drives out demons by power of demons
Matt. 12:25-28	Kingdom devided will fall
Matt. 12:43-45	The return of the evil spirit (Hazard of exorcism without Christ coming in!) (Luke 11:24-26)
Matt. 15:21-28	The daughter of the Syrophoenician woman healed of her demon possession (Mark 7:24-30; DA 399-402)
Matt. 17:14-21	Jesus heals the boy who is demon possessed (Mark 9:14-29; Luke 9:37-43; DA 427-429)
DA 256.5	Jews possessed by same evil spirit as demoniacs
DA 257-259	Modern counterpart of this possession
DA 323.2-324	Control by Satan explained
DA 352.2	Supernatural help assured for His disciples' contact with demons
Mark 1:21-27	Demoniac in the temple (Luke 4:31-37; DA 255, 256)
Mark 1:32-34	Jesus drives out demons in Capernaum
Mark 1:39	Preaching and driving out demons all over Galilee
DA 467.4	Demons forced to confess Christ as the Holy One of God
DA 493.1-3	Christians who think and talk too much about the devil
Mark 3:11, 12	Evil spirits said Jesus was the Son of God (DA 542.0; 579)
Mark 9:38	A non-church member driving out demons in Christ's name (Luke 9:49, 50)
DA 645.1	Judas possessed with a demon (DA 696.1)
DA 679.1	End of Satan's empire determined at the cross
Mark 16:9	Mary, out of whom Jesus cast seven devils (MB 129.2; DA 568)
Mark 16:17	Believers will drive out devils in Jesus' name
DA 717.0	Judas given power from Christ to cast out devils
DA 720.1, 2	The steps to demon possession
DA 733.2	Demons in human form at the trial of Jesus
DA 734.3	Satan led the mob who wanted Jesus to be crucified

DA 746.4	Satan and his angels in human form at the cross
DA 785.1	Priests who crucified Jesus now entirely in Satan's power
DA 823.3	Satan's captives to be delivered
Luke 6:18	Healed of being troubled by evil spirits (Matt. 4:24)
Luke 7:21	Jesus cast out demons as John the Baptist's disciples observed
COL 171.0	Christ accused of being demon possessed (John 7:20; 8:48, 49; 9:20)
COL 236.2	Giving self to the power of Satan
Luke 10:17-20	Even the devils subject to us in Thy name
Luke 13:10-13	Crippled woman who had an evil spirit
John 13:27	Judas finally devil possessed
MB 145.3	Casting out devils apart from Jesus

Satan's original charge was that the law of God could not be obeyed. When man broke the law of God, Satan exulted and added another charge—that man could not be forgiven. He had no idea that God Himself would pay the penalty. But Jesus' life and death proved that sinners could be forgiven and that the law of God can be obeyed, not only by Jesus, but by those who live the life of faith as He did. This twofold message of forgiveness and obedience is the heart of the remnant's mission during the time of the three angels and the final work of Christ in heaven. Jesus as our High Priest provides forgiveness for sinners and power to obey. These two truths are equally necessary. It is extremely important that the remnant people understand this twofold work of Christ in heaven; otherwise, it will be impossible for them to fulfill their mission. Justification by faith (God's work for us) and the righteousness of Christ (which includes God's work in us) are the themes to be presented to a perishing world.

What Jesus Said About the Mismanagement of Church Funds

When the early research and study for this book on what Jesus had to say about current issues was begun, the issues of this chapter were just looming up on the church's financial horizon. As a matter of fact, the last *five* chapters of this book were in preparation at that time. In studying what Jesus had to say about justification, the faith relationship, sanctification, the nature of Christ, and perfection, we discovered more than just what Jesus had to say about those subjects! We also discovered a tremendous truth—Jesus' teachings are up-to-date and give tremendous insights into current problems. Regardless of what issue you happen to be facing at the moment, the teachings of Jesus have something to say to you that is current, fresh, to the point.

Would you like to know what Jesus has to say about the recent revelations about the mismanagement of funds? Have you been one of those who has questioned whether or not it is right to continue giving to and supporting a church after such an episode? Have you perhaps been casting about for an alternate method of contributing your tithes and offerings, rather than bringing it to the church treasuries? Jesus has something to say on the subject!

First consider this insight from the book *Selected Messages,* book 1, page 406: "The trials of the children of Israel, and their attitude just before the first coming of Christ, have been presented before me again and again to illustrate the position of the people of God in their experience before the second coming of Christ—how the enemy sought every occasion to take control of the minds of the Jews, and today he is seeking to blind the minds of God's servants, that they may not be able to discern the precious truth."

This suggests that we can be assured that the lessons and truths to be learned from Christ's day are applicable to us, as we approach the second coming of Christ.

Let's look at this subject under four major headings: First, what was the condition of the church and its financial system at the time of Christ? Second, how did Christ teach His disciples to relate to the financial program of the organized church? Third, what did Jesus teach as the purpose of giving? Fourth, what will be the result of following the teaching and example of Jesus on this subject?

Now to the first point. What was the condition of the church and its financial program at the time of Christ? It was corrupt. The money changers in the temple were in league with the priests and rulers to defraud and extort the people. This resulted in the enrichment of the priests and rulers. The situation is described in *The Desire of Ages,* pages 155 to 157. First, the animals sold for the temple sacrifices were sold at exorbitant prices. And second, the changing of the common currency for the temple coins allowed opportunity for further dishonesty on the part of the money changers. Because of the greed for gain that had become a ruling principle in their lives, the priests and rulers manifested no sympathy or compassion for the poor and suffering who could not pay their way. There is no question but that gross misappropriation of funds took place at the time of Christ's first advent.

The condition of the temple, which had become one vast marketplace, caused Christ to begin His public ministry by cleansing it of the buyers and sellers. Yet at the close of His ministry, at the time of the second cleansing of the temple, conditions at the temple were even worse than before. See page 589.

In light of this corruption and abuse of the system of tithes and offerings and sacrifices that God had appointed, how did Christ teach His followers, by precept and example, to relate to the organized church and its financial needs?

Notice, first of all, Luke 2:22-24. "And when the days of her [Mary's] purification according to the law of Moses were accomplished, they brought him [Jesus] to Jerusalem, to present him to the Lord; (as it is written in the law of the Lord, Every male that

THE MISMANAGEMENT OF CHURCH FUNDS

openeth the womb shall be called holy to the Lord;) And to offer a sacrifice according to that which is said in the law of the Lord, A pair of turtledoves, or two young pigeons." Notice that these offerings were brought *to the temple*.

In Matthew 17:24-28, the story is told of Peter and the temple tax. As you recall, the priests and rulers came to him, hoping to trap his Master by devious means. Impulsive person that he was, Peter agreed that he and Jesus should pay the temple tax. When Jesus became aware of the situation, He told Peter how to obtain the needed coin, and then instructed him to "take, and give unto them for me and thee." Verse 27.

The Pharisees at that time were very careful to retain their reputation for being righteous and exact in their behavior. Every summer they would go out to their gardens, with a great show of ceremony, and make sure that one mint leaf out of ten was set aside as tithe. Jesus spoke of their practice in Matthew 23:23. "Woe unto you, scribes and Pharisees, hypocrites! for ye pay tithe of mint and anise and cummin, and have omitted the weightier matters of the law, judgment, mercy, and faith: these ought ye to have done . . ." A lot of people stop right there! And they say, "That's right. It's being legalistic, it's being pharisaical, to be concerned with tithes and offerings." But the verse doesn't stop there. It goes right on and says, "These ought ye to have done, and not to leave the other undone."

On another occasion, when the Pharisees and rulers were trying to ensnare Jesus, they asked Him whether or not it was lawful to pay tribute to Caesar. See Mark 12:13-17. Jesus replied by asking for a penny. Holding it up for them to see, He asked whose image and inscription was on it. And then He gave the principle for giving that has been accepted ever since by His followers: "Pay to the Emperor what belongs to him"—and the double lesson—"and pay to God what belongs to God." Mark 12:17, TEV.

"Never, by word or deed, did Jesus lessen man's obligation to present gifts and offerings to God. It was Christ who gave all the directions of the law in regard to tithes and offerings. When on earth He commended the poor woman who gave her all to the temple treasury."—*The Desire of Ages,* p. 397.

The incident of the widow who contributed her two mites to the temple treasury took place in the middle of Jesus' last week before His crucifixion. We read about it in Mark 12:41-44. "And Jesus sat over against the treasury, and beheld how the people cast money into the treasury: and many that were rich cast in much. And there came a certain poor widow, and she threw in two mites, which make a farthing. And he called unto him his disciples, and saith unto them, Verily I say unto you, That this poor widow hath cast more in, than all they which have cast into the treasury: for all they did cast in of their abundance; but she of her want did cast in all that she had, even all her living."

Jesus knew of the corruption of the temple financial system. He had already twice cleansed the temple, but to no avail. It would seem that the least He could have done, if the widow really wanted to give away her last few cents, was to advise her to give it to some worthy person or project. But no. He commended her for bringing it to the temple.

"Many would have advised her to keep her pittance for her own use; given into the hands of the well-fed priests, it would be lost sight of among the many costly gifts brought to the treasury. But Jesus understood her motive. She believed the service of the temple to be of God's appointment, and she was anxious to do her utmost to sustain it."—Page 615. "Man's abuse of the gift could not turn God's blessing from the giver."—Page 614.

I am not implying by the foregoing that the Seventh-day Adventist Church is as corrupt as was the Jewish church at the time of Christ. But the comparison enunciates an important principle which should not be overlooked. The principle has to do with what Jesus had to say about how to deal with the mishandling of church funds. If church funds are mishandled, it is our responsibility to make our complaints—to the proper church authorities.

"Some have been dissatisfied and have said: 'I will no longer pay my tithe, for I have no confidence in the way things are managed at the heart of the work.' But will you rob God because you think the management of the work is not right? Make your complaint, plainly and openly, in the right spirit, to the proper ones. Send in your petitions for things to be adjusted and set in order; but do not withdraw from the work of God, and prove unfaithful, because others are not doing right."—*Testimonies*, vol. 9, p. 249.

If we are delegated the responsibility of handling the funds, we must do our utmost to prevent any misuse. But our giving pattern should be unbroken. We make our complaints to the right source, in the right forum, before the proper authorities, in the right spirit—and we keep on giving. We keep on giving, not because we are assured that God's church is free from mistakes, but because, like the widow, we believe in and love the church of God, and also believe in God's power to protect His own interests. We will continue to do our utmost to sustain God's cause because we believe in God's cause and want above all else to see His cause succeed here on earth.

Now let's consider briefly why God invites us to give in the first place. Giving is the law of life for the universe. Sin originated when this law was broken. See *The Desire of Ages,* p. 21. Giving is a result of love, and when we have given our hearts to Jesus, we will also bring our gifts to Him. See page 63. We put our treasure where our hearts are, and the reverse is also true—our heart will be where our treasure is! See Matthew 6:19-21.

Let us consider recent revelations of financial mismanagement for a moment in the light of the foregoing principle. Who will be most concerned with correcting the financial mistakes of the church and preventing their recurrence in the future? Will it be those who have given and have invested their treasure in the church, or those who have not? The answer is obvious.

This brings to mind another purpose God has in view in inviting us not only to give—but to give to *His church*. His church on earth can go forward only as those who belong to that church have invested in it their treasure—and their hearts. God needs His people to commit their talents and means and minds to His cause. Then He will be able to work through us. "Your heart will always be where your riches are." Luke 12:34, TEV.

But above all else, God's purpose in asking us to contribute of our means to His church is for *our* good. The reason God invites us to give is because we need to give. In *Testimonies,* volume 3, page 390, we are told, "Whatever necessity there is for our agency in the advancement of the cause of God, He has purposely arranged for our good." And *Thoughts From the Mount of Blessing,* page 82, says "While he that gives to the needy blesses others, he himself is blessed in a still greater degree. The grace of Christ in the soul is developing traits of character that are the opposite of selfishness,—traits that will refine, ennoble, and enrich the life."

Finally, what will be the result of following the teaching and example of Jesus on this subject? We *will* bring our offerings to God. See *The Desire of Ages,* p. 107. If we have given our hearts to Jesus, we will also bring our gifts to Him. See page 65. And the result will be that our gifts will be effective. That's a promise! Read it in page 65: "The offering from the heart that loves, God delights to honor, giving it highest efficiency in service for Him."

Are you worried that some of *your* means have been lost through recent disclosures of financial mismanagement? Don't be. If you gave because of love for God and His cause, it was not *your* offering that was mismanaged! As in the case of the widow's mites, your offering was honored and given a place of highest efficiency in God's service—that's what God promises you! Apparently there are sufficient funds in the Lord's treasury from other sources, which He uses to make up for the mistakes and failures on the part of those who handle the funds. He continues to protect the gifts of those who love His cause. Perhaps some of our humanistic gimmicks to raise funds have been at the root of our current financial problems and have given the devil a foothold in controlling a portion of the funds in the church treasury. But the offering from the heart that loves is safe. It will accomplish the work for which it was intended. God has made Himself responsible for that, and we can trust Him to fulfill His promise.

Do you love Jesus today? Do you love His church? Do you long to see the gospel message go forward in the world? Then you can safely bring your gifts to His treasury, knowing that they will be given the highest efficiency in service for Him.

Mishandling of Church Funds

DA 21:2	Giving is the law of life for the universe
DA 21.3	Sin began when this law was broken
Luke 2:22-24	Jesus' parents brought offering *to the temple* (DA 50.2)
DA 63:1	Wise men gave their hearts—then their gifts to Jesus
DA 65.2	The offering from the heart that loves is given highest efficiency
	If we have given our hearts, we *will* bring our gifts

THE MISMANAGEMENT OF CHURCH FUNDS 121

Matt. 6:19-21	Your heart is where your riches are (Luke 12:34)
DA 107.3	Those who are truly Christ's will bring their offerings to God
DA 155.1-3	Misappropriation of funds at the time of Christ
DA 156.1	Abuses of temple monies
DA 157.1, 2	*Christ* to cleanse the unholy traffic
DA 163.4	Sin of desecrating the temple was largely that of the priests
DA 168.1	Nicodemus and many others distressed with temple corruption
Matt. 17:24-28	Jesus pays the temple tax
Matt. 19:21-23	Rich young ruler—it's hard for rich men! (Mark 10:17-31; Luke 18:18-30)
Matt. 23:23	These ought ye to have done and not left the other undone (Luke 11:42)
DA 397.1	Never by word or deed did Christ lessen man's obligation to give tithes and offerings to God
DA 433.4	Peter and the temple tax
Mark 11:15-19	Second cleansing of temple (Matt. 21:12-17; Luke 19:45-48; DA 589.1)
Mark 12:13-17	Pay to God what is God's (DA 602.2)
DA 614.3	Man's abuse of the gift could not turn God's blessing from the giver
Mark 12:41-44	The widow's offering (Luke 21:1-4; DA 614-616)
DA 616.3-617	The duty of bringing tithes and offerings
COL 300.3	God's purpose for tithes and offerings, then and now
MB 82.2	God's purpose for our giving is *our* good (MB 90.1)

Satan's original charge was that the law of God could not be obeyed. When man broke the law of God, Satan exulted and added another charge–that man could not be forgiven. He had no idea that God Himself would pay the penalty. But Jesus' life and death proved that sinners could be forgiven and that the law of God can be obeyed, not only by Jesus, but by those who live the life of faith as He did. This twofold message of forgiveness and obedience is the heart of the remnant's mission during the time of the three angels and the final work of Christ in heaven. Jesus as our High Priest provides forgiveness for sinners and power to obey. These two truths are equally necessary. It is extremely important that the remnant people understand this twofold work of Christ in heaven; otherwise, it will be impossible for them to fulfill their mission. Justification by faith (God's work for us) and the righteousness of Christ (which includes God's work in us) are the themes to be presented to a perishing world.

What Jesus Said About the Atonement

Have you ever heard of an airline pilot who didn't believe in flying? Have you met a doctor who doesn't think health is important? Do you know of any fish that believe water is unnecessary? Let me ask you one more question: Do you know of any Chritians who no longer believe that Christ died for their sins? To that last question many of us would have to answer Yes.

Perhaps one of the greatest signs that the end is just upon us is the fact that we've stopped focusing on the peripheral issues, such as whether or not it's OK to go bowling, drink cola beverages, or take a shower Sabbath morning. Suddenly, the discussions and controversies are centering around the basic tenets of our faith. Perhaps the devil is beginning to realize that his time is short, so he's going for the jugular vein. But the shift in recent times has been very marked. Until a few years ago, some things were taken for granted, unchallenged. But no more. We have been forced to examine and scrutinize our most basic, fundamental doctrines and beliefs.

One of the most recent dialogues has been concerning the atonement of Christ. Some are saying that it was unnecessary. It was incidental. God could have forgiven man without the cross, without the death of Christ. Christ died a martyr's death, nothing more. They contend that our former concept of the atonement and death of Christ for our sin is a pagan idea.

Some recent Sabbath School lessons on the subject of the atonement caused considerable discussion and controversy as Seventh-day Adventists Christians everywhere began to examine this most basic belief of Christendom. Do we believe in the need for the shedding of blood for the remission of sins? Do we accept the necessity of the cross? Or is the idea of a sacrifice a hangover from heathen beliefs and not a valid Christian doctrine?

Because of space limitations we cannot study this subject as thoroughly as I would like. But I shall do the best I can in the limited space available. Consider with me some things that Jesus had to say about the subject of His own death and its purpose. Once again, the life and teachings of Christ bring positive, definite light on the current controversies, giving us assurance and certainty in the current issues of the church.

Let's take a deeper look at the issues involved in the cross. What was it that broke the heart of Jesus? Why did He die? Was the cross really a vital part of the plan of salvation?

The concept that Christ died for our sins is an old, old concept. It is found throughout Scripture. From the earliest record of human activity after the fall—Adam and Eve coming to the entrance of the Garden of Eden to offer the morning and evening sacrifices—to the final, triumphant "marriage supper of the *Lamb*" in the earth made new, the symbol of the death of Christ is uplifted.

Paul, who was a champion of the cross, said in 1 Corinthians 15:3, "Christ died for our sins according to the scriptures." And he also said in Romans 3:26 that God is just and the justifier of those who believe in Jesus. So let's turn to the life and teachings of Christ and see what Jesus had to say about the atonement.

1. The angel said in Matthew 1:21, "Thou shalt call his name JESUS: for he shall save his people from their sins." In Luke 19:10 Jesus said, "For the Son of man is come to seek and to save that which was lost." The thesis of the Christian religion, that which distinguishes it from all other religions, is the belief that mankind needs a Saviour. Man cannot save himself. That has been the basis of the Christian religion from its very inception.

We are invited to study the cross and its significance. "The cross of Calvary is to be lifted high above the people, absorbing their minds and concentrating their thoughts."—*Thoughts From the Mount of Blessing,* p. 44. "The study of the incarnation of Christ, His atoning sacrifice and mediatorial work, will employ the mind of the diligent student as long as time shall last."—

Christ's Object Lessons, p. 134. "Both the redeemed and the unfallen beings will find in the cross of Christ their science and their song."—*The Desire of Ages,* pp. 19, 20. The attention of the people must be directed to Christ's great sacrifices. See page 485. Christ desired to call attention to the sacrifice that was to crown His mission to a fallen world as the Lamb of God. See page 571.

2. Let's go on to Matthew 26:26-28. "And as they were eating, Jesus took bread, and blessed it, and brake it, and gave it to the disciples, and said, Take, eat; this is my body. And he took the cup, and gave thanks, and gave it to them, saying, Drink ye all of it; for this is my blood of the new testament, which is shed for many for the remission of sins." If the cross of Christ was to go, then what would be the significance of the Lord's Supper? It would have to go too, wouldn't it?

Let's look at one or two references from the inspired commentary. Here is what the first one says: "To the death of Christ we owe even this earthly life."—*The Desire of Ages,* p. 660. But spiritual life also is dependent upon Christ's sacrifice. See pages 660, 661. "The Lord's Supper was given to commemorate the great deliverance wrought out as the result of the death of Christ."—Pages 652, 653.

3. Was the cross of Christ essential, or just incidental? In Luke 24:25, 26 we find an interesting conversation that took place on the road to Emmaus. Notice: "Then he said upon them, O fools, and slow of heart to believe all that the prophets have spoken: ought not Christ to have suffered these things, and to enter into his glory?" Verse 46: "And he said unto them, Thus it is written, and thus it behoved Christ to suffer, and to rise from the dead the third day." John 3:14 says, "As Moses lifted up the serpent in the wilderness, even so *must* the Son of man be lifted up." Emphasis supplied.

And the inspired commentary on that says, "Only by His death could the world be saved."—*The Desire of Ages,* p. 622. Remission of sins is found only in the merits of Christ. Christ's mission is fulfilled only through suffering. He must bear the sins of the whole world. See pages 129, 806.

Only through dying could Jesus impart life to men. Nothing less than the death of Christ could make His love efficacious for us. His sacrifice is the center of our hope. See pages 388, 660.

The guilt of fallen humanity Jesus must bear; as a man He must suffer the consequences of man's sin. See page 686.

This doesn't sound like Christ's vicarious death was an option, does it? Rather, it is a vital necessity in the plan for man's salvation from sin.

4. The Bible says that God was in Christ, reconciling the world unto Himself. See 2 Corinthians 5:19. Some people have said, "Do you mean that God was angry and looking for blood to appease His wrath?" No, not at all. The problem is, as it is expressed in Isaiah 53:4 (TEV), that "all the while we thought that his suffering was punishment sent by God." Did God look down on the world of sin and say, "I want a pound of flesh; I want to see some blood"? Is that the way it was? No! God was in Christ, reconciling the world unto Himself. The Father and the Son were together in the sacrifice for man's redemption. Jesus said, "I and my Father are one." John 10:30. From God's own love comes the gift that reconciles us to Him. See *The Desire of Ages,* p. 113. God "sacrificed Himself, in Christ, for man's redemption."—Page 762.

Is the concept of the atonement pagan and heathen? Well, there is an *interpretation* of the atonement that is of pagan origin. If we think that God the Father needed to be appeased, then we have a heathen concept of the atonement. Or if we think of offering some gift of our own to reconcile us to Him, *that* is also a heathen concept. It was Cain's offering, the fruit of his own labors, that was an offense to God and distorted the symbolism of the sacrificial system. Micah 6:7 asks this question: "Shall I give my firstborn for my transgression, the fruit of my body for the sin of my soul?" *That's* pagan. The Christian belief accepts the sacrifice made *for* us, not *by* us, as the ground and means for salvation and reconciliation with God.

5. Human reasoning is incapable of understanding the mystery of the atonement. Look at Matthew 16:21-23. "From that time forth began Jesus to shew unto his disciples, how that he must go unto Jerusalem, and suffer many things of the elders and chief priests and scribes, and be killed, and be raised again the third day. Then Peter took him, and began to rebuke him, saying, Be it

far from thee, Lord: this shall not be unto thee. But he turned, and said unto Peter, Get thee behind me, Satan: thou art an offence unto me: for thou savourest not the things that be of God, but those that be of men." Peter didn't like the idea of the cross. Notice the comment in *The Desire of Ages,* pages 415, 416: "Peter did not desire to see the cross in the work of Christ. The impression which his words would make was directly opposed to that Christ desired to make on the minds of His followers, and the Saviour was moved to utter one of the sternest rebukes that ever fell from His lips." When we get into the subject of the atonement, we are grappling with something bigger than we are, and there's no one smart enough. Yet we are invited to try. Human science is too limited to comprehend the atonement. It is a mistake to put our feeble human judgment above the Bible truth on this subject. See *Christ's Object Lessons,* p. 39.

I read a book recently in which the idea of the necessity and importance of the cross was downgraded. The primary authority for the book, as I perceived it, was the author's own logic and reason and judgment. The idea of the cross did not make sense to his human understanding. And if we find ourselves in that position, we might do well to take a lesson from the experience of Peter.

6. Jesus predicted that in the end of time there would be false prophets and false messiahs. See Matthew 24:24. Now I'd like to ask you a question: Does a person have to claim to be the messiah falsely in order to be a false messiah, or is it possible to have false ideas about the Messiah and end up doing equal service to the enemy, who would like to do away with the cross? Could not this warning, which was given specifically for the last days to help prevent the devil from deceiving the very elect, have special meaning for any device of the enemy to detract from the true Messiah and His mission?

Let's read one reference, *The Desire of Ages,* page 317: "The Jews had been instructed from childhood concerning the work of the Messiah. The inspired utterances of patriarchs and prophets and the symbolic teaching of the sacrificial service had been theirs. But they had disregarded the light; and now they saw in Jesus nothing to be desired." The same is true today. Those who disregard the truth of Christ's sacrifice will ultimately reject Christ Himself.

7. Turn to Matthew 26:52-54: "Then said Jesus unto him, Put up again thy sword into his place: for all they that take the sword shall perish with the sword. Thinkest thou that I cannot now pray to my Father, and he shall presently give me more than twelve legions of angels? But how then shall the scriptures be fulfilled, that thus *it must be.*" Emphasis supplied.

The cross was not incidental in Christ's life; it was His ultimate purpose in coming to this earth. Now go to Matthew 27:39-42. "And they that passed by reviled him, wagging their heads, and saying, Thou that destroyest the temple, and buildest it in three days, save thyself. If thou be the Son of God, come down from the cross. Likewise also the chief priests mocking him, with the scribes and elders, said, He saved others; himself he cannot save. If he be the King of Israel, let him now come down from the cross, and we will believe him."

When someone comes along today and uses some maneuver to try to do away with the significance and meaning of the death of Christ on the cross as our substitute, we can see reenacted in a modern setting what the multitude of mockers said at the foot of the cross, "Let him come down from the cross, and we will believe him."

What is the result of seeing Christ on the cross? Notice the following two references: When we see Christ upon the cross, "self will no longer clamor to be recognized."—*The Desire of Ages*, p. 439. "Pride and self-worship cannot flourish in the soul that keeps fresh in memory the scenes of Calvary."—Page 661.

Could this be one reason why the enemy tries so hard to get rid of the cross? Ponder it for a moment. If a proud person does not like to admit that his human reasoning is inadequate to comprehend the cross, and if a proud person is not willing for self to be humbled, then he will have to get rid of the cross. Pride and self-worship cannot stay in the heart that keeps fresh in memory the scenes of Calvary.

8. If you choose to get rid of the cross, the larger portion of the Old Testament has to go as well. In John 3:14, 15 Jesus made the analogy between the uplifted serpent in the wilderness and His

THE ATONEMENT   129

own sacrifice. John the Baptist referred to Jesus as "the Lamb of God" when he said, "Behold the Lamb of God, which taketh away the sin of the world." John 1:29. The entire sacrificial system pointed to the death of Christ for man's sin. See *The Desire of Ages,* p. 165. Christ was the way when Abel presented to God the blood of the slain lamb, representing the blood of the Redeemer. See page 663.

Another interesting Old Testament analogy of the death of Christ was the experience of Abraham and Isaac. You will remember that Abraham was asked to offer Isaac as a burnt offering. At the final, crucial moment an angel stayed the hand of Abraham, and Isaac's life was spared. There are those who would think that this experience was typical of Christ. They are saying that, in reality, Christ did not die—and thus it is a mistake to believe in His "death" for the sins of man. But if that were true, then Isaac would have been a type of Christ. Read *The Desire of Ages,* pages 112, 113. The experience on Mount Moriah did indeed point forward to Christ, but Isaac was not the representative of the Saviour. A ram, caught in the thicket, which God Himself provided, was offered as the sacrifice. The ram represented Jesus; Isaac did not.

9. For yet another of Christ's teaching on the subject of His sacrifice, turn to John 10. "I am the door: by me if any man enter in, he shall be saved, and shall go in and out, and find pasture." "I am the good shepherd: the good shepherd *giveth his life for the sheep.*" "As the Father knoweth me, even so know I the Father: and *I lay down my life for the sheep.* And other sheep I have, which are not of this fold: them also I must bring, and they shall hear my voice; and there shall be one fold, and one shepherd. Therefore doth my Father love me, because I lay down my life, that I might take it again." Verses 9, 11, 15-17. Emphasis supplied.

This reminds us of the prophecy of Christ in Isaiah 53, which is full of predictions concerning the sufferings of Christ. Have you read it lately? He was brought as a lamb to the slaughter. He was wounded for our transgressions. He was bruised for our iniquities. *The Desire of Ages,* page 458, speaks of Isaiah's prediction of Christ's sufferings and death.

10. In John 12 we find the experience of the Greeks who came to see Jesus. Jesus told them that the hour was come that the Son of man should be glorified. See verse 23. Then He explained in verses 24 and 27: "Verily, verily, I say unto you, Except a corn of wheat fall into the ground and die, it abideth alone: but if it die, it bringeth forth much fruit." "Now is my soul troubled; and what shall I say? Father, save me for this hour: but *for this cause came I unto this hour.*" Emphasis supplied.

There's a lot of glory connected with the cross. And if the devil hates the glory of Christ, then he's going to hate the cross, isn't he? And it is a tragedy that any thinking could arise among Seventh-day Adventists that would do away with the glory of the cross.

Jesus chose not to abide alone. Rather, He accepted the furrow of death that He might bring forth much fruit.

It is spoken of again in John 11:49, 50, coming, of all places, from the lips of the haughty Caiaphas. His very words were haughty! He said, "Ye know nothing at all, nor consider that it is expedient for us, that one man should die for the people, and that the whole nation perish not."

Then in verses 51 John explains: "This spake he not of himself: but being high priest that year, he prophesied that Jesus should die for that nation; and not for that nation only, but that also he should gather together in one the children of God that were scattered abroad."

It is expedient for us that Jesus died. We can say it without the curled lip of Caiaphas, without the gravel that he had in his throat. It is expedient for us that one Man die. Do you still believe that? It's what the Bible teaches on the subject.

11. In John 20:17 Jesus told Mary Magdaline that He was not yet ascended to His Father. *The Desire of Ages,* page 790, tells why He was to ascend to His Father at that time. "Jesus refused to receive the homage of His people until He had the assurance that His sacrifice was accepted by the Father. He ascended to the heavenly courts, and from God Himself heard the assurance that His atonement for the sins of men had been ample, that through His blood all might gain eternal life. The Father ratified the covenant made with Christ, that He would receive repen-

tant and obedient men, and would love them even as He loves His Son."

If you just took that experience all by itself, you might be inclined to accept the idea that God was looking for a pound of flesh. But if you look at the larger picture, and piece together all of the evidence, it becomes apparent that this was not so. God was in Christ reconciling the world unto Himself.

12. There is a great controversy involved in the story of the cross. John 12:31-33 talks about it. Jesus was speaking as He faced the sacrifice He was about to make, "Now is the judgment of this world: now shall the prince of this world be cast out. And I, if I be lifted up from the earth, will draw all men unto me. This he said, signifying what death he should die."

There is one particular chapter in *The Desire of Ages* that speaks of the great controversy factor in the death of Christ. It's the chapter entitled "It Is Finished." The entire chapter is permeated with truth on this vital subject. I would urge you to read it prayerfully. But the great controversy factor is conspicuously absent from the material presented by those who desire to do away with the necessity for the cross and the atonement of Christ.

13. There was justice involved in the death of Christ. God believes in justice, and we can be thankful for that. God's government is based on laws. Justice is essential for government, for a government can endure only so long as it has laws that are just. No government is any stronger than its laws. And no law is any stronger than the penalty for breaking that law. And no penalty is any stronger than the enforcement of that penalty. The parent who looks up the stairs and says, "This is the last time I'm going to say 'this is the last time,' " has already lost the battle.

God is the originator of justice; it is an integral part of His character. Because the law could not be set aside, because the penalty could not be set aside, and because the enforcement of the penalty could not be set aside, His justice had to be met.

When Satan found himself outside of the gates of heaven, he was Exhibit A that God is a God of justice. But what Satan did not understand was that God is also a God of mercy. So the devil came up with what he considered to be a clever plot. He would get man to sin and thus try again to prove that God's laws could not be kept. And then, because of God's justice, man would also find himself outside of the heavenly gates.

Then, Satan reasoned, either God will have to forgive us all and take us all back into His kingdom, or else I will have a kingdom of my own, the kingdom of mankind, to rule according to my own wishes.

What he did not know was that there was a plan, devised from times eternal (see Romans 16:25 and 1 Samuel 14:14), whereby man could be given an opportunity to be freed from Satan's dominion. Jesus came to this earth and by His life and death proved that God is a God both of justice and mercy, and that justice does not destroy mercy any more than mercy destroys justice.

Matthew 20:27-28 says, "Whosoever will be chief among you, let him be your servant: even as the Son of man came not to be ministered unto, but to minister, and to give his life a *ransom* for many." Emphasis supplied. Those who want to do away with the cross don't like the idea of a ransom, but it is a Bible teaching. And there is much support in the inspired commentary as well. Jesus, "the Sin Bearer, endures the wrath of divine justice, and for thy sake becomes sin itself."—*The Desire of Ages*, p. 26. "As substitute and surety for sinful man, Christ was suffering under divine justice."—Page 686. And when Christ was accepted again into the courts of heaven after the ascension, "the voice of God is heard proclaiming that justice is satisfied."—Page 834.

"It was to atone for man's transgression of the law that Christ laid down His life. Could the law have been changed or set aside, then Christ need not have died. By His life on earth He honored the law of God. By his death He established it. He gave His life as a sacrifice, not to destroy God's law, not to create a lower standard, but that justice might be maintained, that the law might be shown to be immutable, that it might stand fast forever."—*Christ's Object Lessons*, p. 314.

14. There were even bigger issues involved in Christ's sacrifice on the cross than those which concern our own world. The entire universe was involved. Revelation 12, of course, talks about the accuser being cast down. "But the work of human redemption was not all that is accomplished by the cross. The love of God is manifested to the universe. The prince of this world is cast out.

The accusations which Satan has brought against God are refuted. The reproach which he has cast upon heaven is forever removed. Angels as well as men are drawn to the Redeemer. 'I, if I be lifted up from the earth,' He said, 'Will draw all men unto Me.' "—*The Desire of Ages,* p. 626.

15. The story of the prodigal son was not given to teach the atonement. We are told repeatedly that this parable was given to show how God receives the repenting sinner who returns to Him. (See *Christ's Object Lessons,* p. 198, for example.) One cannot base his theology of no-atonement-needed on a parable that wasn't given to teach about the atonement, at the same time ignoring the tremendous mountain of evidence the other direction. The teachings of Jesus clearly show the truth that Christ died for our sins, according to Scripture. It is the foundation and basis of the entire Christian faith. It is not only taught in the teachings of Christ, which we have examined here in detail, but it is found throughout all of the Bible.

In conclusion, I'd like to list briefly several things that were accomplished by Christ's death on the cross. (1) He proved that God's love for man is great. (2) He paid the penalty for sin. (3) He proved that the law could not be changed or set aside. (4) He proved that the penalty for sin was fair and just. (5) He proved the awfulness of sin. (6) He purchased the right to destroy the devil. (7) He purchased the right to forgive the sinner and still be just. (8) He made grace available to all who believe and trust in Him. (9) He redeemed us from the curse of the law. (10) He obtained the keys to the grave, the right to raise the dead. (11) He proved that the wages of sin is death. (12) He made the Sabbath a memorial of creation *and* redemption. (13) He vindicated the character of God before the universe. (14) He proved that God's government would stand forever. (15) He bought back the lost dominion.

No wonder it will be proclaimed, "Worthy is the Lamb that was slain to receive power, and riches, and wisdom, and strength, and honour, and glory, and blessing." Revelation 5:12. Wouldn't you like to join with "both the redeemed and the unfallen beings [who] will find in the cross of Christ their science and their song" throughout all of eternity? See *The Desire of Ages,* p. 20.

The Atonement
(God is just and justifier—Romans 3)

John 3:14, 15	Son of man must be lifted up to secure eternal life for humanity (SD 174.3)
John 10:9	Jesus is the door for salvation
John 10:11, 15, 17	Jesus is willing to die for the sheep
DA 484.1	Christ bore the sin of the world, yielded His life as a sacrifice for us
John 12:24, 27	A seed dies to produce many (DA 622.2-623.4)
DA 622.2	Only by His death could the world be saved
John 12:31-34	Satan overthrown by Jesus' death (DA 624.4)
John 12:27	"For this cause I came"
DA 694.1	Christ tasted the sufferings of death for every man (DA 686.4)
John 11:50	Better for one man to die for the people (John 18:14)
Matt. 27:42	He saved others, Himself He cannot save
DA 749.1	If He comes down from the cross we will believe! (Matt. 27:40-42)
DA 762.4	By His death Jesus proved that sin could be forgiven
DA 761.4	GC factor in the atonement—the prosecution
DA 762.3	God's love expressed in His justice no less than in His mercy
DA 759.5	Gethsemane sorrow exceeded the last struggle with death
DA 762.1	God sacrificed Himself in Christ for man's redemption
DA 772.2	Jesus slain by the sin of the world (DA 774.2)
DA 790.3	Father assured Jesus that the atonement was accepted
Luke 24:26	Necessary for Messiah to suffer these things
DA 821.0, 1	Forgiveness through Christ alone
Matt. 20:28	Son of man to give His life a ransom for many
Matt. 26:28	This is My blood poured out for many for the forgiveness of sin
Matt. 26:54	If angels deliver Me, how could the Scriptures come true which say this is what *must* happen?
Mark 10:45	The Son of man came to give His life to redeem many people
Mark 13:22	False messiahs will appear
Luke 19:10	Son of man came to seek and to save the lost
Luke 22:20	This is My blood which is poured out for you
Luke 24:46	The Messiah must suffer and rise from death
John 6:51	The bread that I will give him is My flesh, which I give so that the world may live
John 10:15-17	"I lay down my life for the sheep"
John 12:24	A grain of wheat must fall into the ground and die
John 12:32	When I am lifted up, I will draw all unto Me
SC 19.1	Not enough merely to perceive the love of God. Only one answer to sin. Behold the Lamb of God who takes away the sin of the world
SC 26.2	We can no more repent without the Spirit of God than we can be pardoned without Christ

THE ATONEMENT

SC 27.1	As we behold Christ whom our sins have pierced, we are led to exclaim, "What is sin, that it should require such a sacrifice? Was all this demanded that we might not perish?"
SC 29.0	The blood of Christ *alone* can cleanse from sin and renew our hearts
SC 31.2	Exceeding sinfulness of sin estimated only in light of the cross. No other way in which man could be saved. Christ took upon Himself our guilt and suffered in our stead because without His sacrifice it was impossible for the human race to escape the defiling power of sin.
SC 32.1	Calvary stands as a memorial of the amazing sacrifice required to atone for the transgression of divine law
SC 36.0	Christ died that we might be forgiven. The merits of His sacrifice are sufficient to present to the Father in our behalf
SC 74.0	Jesus is presenting before God the merits of His blood in remembrance of the price He paid for His redeemed
SC 91.2	God gave His Son to die for man
MB 44.2	Cross of Calvary to be uplifted and absorb the mind
MB 66.2	We have nothing that was not purchased for us by the blood of Christ
COL 39.1	The folly of setting up our judgment over that of the Bible's plain teaching
COL 58.0	Saved by Christ's sacrifice
COL 120.0	Christ bore humiliation, suffering, and death that we might not perish
COL 134.0	Study of Christ's atoning sacrifice will employ the mind as long as time shall last
COL 156.2	Christ offered up His broken body to purchase back God's heritage
COL 176.2	Christ paid an infinite price for the souls of earth's inhabitants
COL 198.2	In the parable of the prodigal son is presented the Lord's dealing with those who have once known the Father's love, but who have allowed the tempter to lead them captive
COL 326.1	All are bought with an infinite price
DA 806.3	Remission of sins found only in the merits of Christ
DA 20.0	Both the redeemed and the unfallen will find in the cross of Christ their science and song
DA 25.2	Christ was condemned for our sins, suffered the death that was ours
DA 25.3	Christ was given to bear our sins, to die as our sacrifice, to become forever one of the human family
DA 52.3	Jesus to pay the ransom for the sins of the whole world
DA 82.3	Jesus to be offered up for the sins of the world
DA 112.5	Abraham's sacrifice on Mount Moriah, a symbol of Him who was to die for the sins of men—ram in place of Israel!
DA 113.0	From God's own love comes the gift that reconciles us to Him. *Ram* represented Jesus—Isaac did *not!*
DA 129.3	Christ's mission fulfilled only through suffering—He must bear the sins of the whole world
DA 142.2	Christ's joy is in seeing souls redeemed by His sacrifice

WHAT JESUS SAID ABOUT

DA 148.4	Wine at marriage feast at Cana a symbol of Christ's death for the sins of the world
DA 165.3	Entire plan of sacrificial worship a foreshadowing of the Saviour's death to save the world
DA 191.1	Our Saviour longs for the love of those He has purchased with His own blood
DA 212.0	In every sacrifice Christ's death was shown
DA 317.2	Those who disregard the truth of Christ's sacrifice ultimately reject Christ Himself
DA 329.0	The Sinless One has taken our place
DA 388.2	Only through dying could He impart life to men
DA 415.3, 4	Peter did not want to see the cross in the work of Christ—and as a result received one of Christ's sternest rebukes, "Get thee behind me, Satan." (See Matthew 16:21-23.)
DA 439.3	When we see Christ crucified, self will no longer clamor for recognition
DA 458.2	Isaiah 53 predicted Christ's sufferings and death
DA 469.2	Son of God alone can bear the guilt of the world—pagan system of sacrifice is to offer up *your own works*
DA 484.0	The Father loves Jesus even more for giving His life to redeem us and taking our transgressions
DA 485.2, 3	The attention of the people must be directed to His great sacrifice
DA 571.2	Christ desired to call attention to the sacrifice that was to crown His mission to a fallen world as the Lamb of God
DA 626.1	*More* than human redemption accomplished at the cross
DA 643.2	Christ knew the sacrifice He must make and for how many it would be in vain
DA 653.0	Lord's Supper given to commemorate the great deliverance resulting from the death of Christ
DA 660.1	Nothing less than the death of Christ could make His love efficacious to us. His sacrifice is the center of our hope.
DA 660.3	To the death of Christ we owe even this earthly life
DA 660.4-661.0	Spiritual life dependent on Christ's sacrifice Pride and self-worship cannot flourish in the soul that keeps fresh in memory the scenes of Calvary
DA 663.3	Christ was the way when Abel presented to God the blood of the slain lamb, representing the blood of the Redeemer
DA 685.2	The guilt of fallen humanity He must bear
DA 686.2	As *man* He must suffer the consequences of man's sin
DA 723.2	Christ was the real Passover lamb
DA 743.2	Jesus was to be crucified for the sins of men
DA 750.1	The dying thief sees Jesus as the Lamb of God
DA 756.0	The Sin Bearer endured the wrath of divine justice—substitution
COL 169.0	With the mighty argument of the cross Christ silences the accuser of the brethren
COL 314.2	Christ gave His life as a sacrifice that justice might be maintained and God's law stand forever
DA 26.2	Through Christ's redeeming work God's government stands justified

THE ATONEMENT

DA 834.3	God proclaims that justice is satisfied
DA 58.1	The cross clears God before the universe for the blame of sin's existence or continuance
COL 157.1	Christ pledged Himself our substitute and surety
DA 686.4	As substitute and surety for sinful man, Christ suffered under divine justice
DA 741.2	Christ our substitute
DA 753.1	Christ our substitute and surety
Matt. 1:21	He will save His people from their sins